THE DIVINE PATTERNS OF

BIBLICAL TAROT

EXPERIENCE THE TRANSFORMATIVE POWER OF FAITH

KRASIMIR KALIN

Table of Contents

Table of Contents

Chapter 6

CHAPTER 1

Introduction to the Biblical Tarot

In the tapestry of human spirituality and reflection, few threads are as richly colored and intricately woven as those of the Tarot and the Christian Bible. Both are ancient, steeped in history, mystery, and a profound depth of symbolic meaning. The Tarot, with its enigmatic archetypes and esoteric wisdom, has guided seekers on their personal journeys of enlightenment and self-discovery for centuries. The Bible, a foundational text of spiritual guidance, moral teachings, and allegorical narratives, has shaped the faith, ethics, and lives of billions. The fusion of these two realms into the Biblical Tarot offers a unique path to insight, blending the introspective depth of the Tarot with the spiritual and moral richness of the Bible.

THE VISION BEHIND THE BIBLICAL TAROT

The Biblical Tarot is more than a deck of cards; it is a bridge between worlds, a dialogue between the soul and the sacred. Its creation was inspired by the desire to make the wisdom of the Tarot accessible to those who find their spiritual home within the Christian tradition, as well as to invite lovers of the Tarot into a new realm of biblical contemplation and reflection. This deck is a tool for guidance, education, and spiritual exploration, designed to resonate with the familiar stories and figures of the Bible while unlocking the archetypal mysteries of the Tarot.

STRUCTURE AND SYMBOLISM

Each card in the Biblical Tarot is a carefully crafted amalgam of traditional Tarot symbolism and biblical narratives. The Major Arcana, representing the major themes and lessons of life, are paired with pivotal biblical stories and characters that embody these archetypes. For instance, "The Fool" is represented by the Soul, embarking on the ultimate journey of knowledge and self-discovery. "The Lovers" is depicted by Adam and Eve, symbolizing choice, morality, and the complexity of human relationships.

The Minor Arcana, reflecting the challenges and experiences of everyday life, are infused with the daily lives, struggles, and triumphs of biblical figures. These cards are drawing from the deep wells of love, betrayal, and forgiveness found in the stories of Samson and Delilah or Ruth and Naomi.

PURPOSE AND USE

The Biblical Tarot is designed for reflection, prayer, and guidance. It invites users to explore their life's journey through the lens of biblical wisdom, offering insights that are at once deeply personal and universally spiritual. Whether used for personal meditation, group study, or spiritual counseling, the Biblical Tarot is a tool for exploring the intersections of life's questions with the timeless teachings of the Bible.

NAVIGATING THIS JOURNEY TOGETHER

This introductory chapter has laid the groundwork for what promises to be a profound journey of discovery. As we turn the pages, we will explore each card in depth, uncovering the rich tapestry of symbolism, story, and spiritual insight that the Biblical Tarot offers. Our journey will take us through the Major and Minor Arcana, delving into the biblical narratives that illuminate each card's meaning and exploring the ways in which these ancient wisdoms speak to the challenges and questions of modern life.

Welcome to the Biblical Tarot, a journey of reflection, discovery, and spiritual growth. Let us embark on this path together, with open hearts and minds, ready to explore the wisdom of the Tarot and the Bible as never before.

CHAPTER 2

How to Use
the Biblical Tarot

The Biblical Tarot, an integration of the profound wisdom found in the Christian Bible with the symbolic depth of the Tarot, serves as a unique tool for spiritual reflection, guidance, and personal growth. This chapter will guide you on how to use these cards, whether you are seeking answers to specific questions, looking for daily inspiration, or delving into deeper spiritual study.

SETTING THE SPACE

Before you begin your consultation with the Biblical Tarot, it is important to create a conducive environment—one that is quiet, comfortable, and free of distractions. Some users prefer to light candles or incense, play soft music, or pray to invite a sense of sacredness into the space. The key is to create an atmosphere that enhances your focus and receptivity to the insights the cards might offer.

FORMULATING YOUR QUESTION

The nature of your question can significantly influence the guidance you receive. While the Biblical Tarot can offer insight into a wide range of queries, from practical dilemmas to spiritual journeys, it is best to ask open-ended questions. Instead of asking *"Will I get the job?"* consider asking, *"What can I do to align myself with my career aspirations?"* This approach invites deeper reflection and actionable insights.

CHOOSING YOUR SPREAD

A "spread" refers to the pattern in which you lay out the cards. Different spreads can be used to explore different types of questions and themes. We will explore this topic in more detail in the next chapter, but here are a few to get started:

- **The One-Card Draw:** *Ideal for daily inspiration or a quick insight. Ask your question or request guidance for the day as you draw a single card.*

- **The Three-Card Spread:** *Represents past, present, and future. It can be used to reflect on the trajectory of a situation or to understand the dynamics at play.*

- **The Five-Card Cross Spread:** *Offers a more comprehensive view, touching on potential challenges, influences, and outcomes related to your question.*

DRAWING THE CARDS

With your question in mind and your chosen spread laid out, shuffle the deck while focusing on your query. Some prefer to shuffle until it feels right to stop; others shuffle a specific number of times. When you feel ready, draw the number of cards your spread requires.

INTERPRETING THE CARDS

Each card in the Biblical Tarot combines traditional Tarot meanings with biblical stories and themes. Begin by examining the card's imagery and the biblical story it represents. Reflect on the themes of the story or character and how they might relate to your question or situation. Refer to the "Study Guide" or this book for additional card information.

APPLICATION AND REFLECTION

The Biblical Tarot is not just about prediction but more about reflection and guidance. Once you have interpreted the cards, consider how the insights apply to your life. What actions can you take? What changes in perspective might be helpful? The goal is to use the cards as a mirror for your soul, reflecting back to you the wisdom and guidance you seek.

KEEPING A JOURNAL

Many find it beneficial to keep a journal of their Tarot readings. Recording your questions, the cards drawn, your interpretations, and any actions you plan to take can be incredibly useful. Over time, this journal can become a valuable resource for personal growth and spiritual reflection.

CLOSING THE SESSION

After your reading, take a moment to thank God, the universe, or your own inner wisdom for the guidance received. Reflect on the experience, and if you've used any special items (like candles or incense), carefully put them away.

ETHICAL CONSIDERATIONS

Remember, the Biblical Tarot is a tool for personal and spiritual growth, not a substitute for professional advice in legal, financial, or health matters. Use it as a way to reflect on your path, make decisions aligned with your highest good, and deepen your understanding of the biblical teachings that resonate with your journey.

By approaching the Biblical Tarot with an open heart and mind, you invite not only insight and guidance but also a deeper connection with the spiritual wisdom that has guided countless seekers throughout history.

CHAPTER 3

Spreads

1

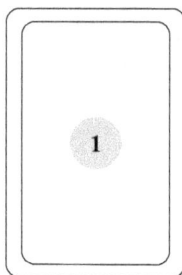

Single Card Spread

The Single Card Spread, in its simplicity and focus, offers a powerful tool for daily inspiration, clarity on a specific question, or a moment of reflection. This spread is particularly useful for those new to the Biblical Tarot, as it allows for a deep dive into the symbolism and message of one card at a time, fostering a gradual and intimate understanding of the deck.

FORMULATING YOUR INTENTION OR QUESTION

While the Single Card Spread can be used without a specific question, focusing your thoughts can help in receiving a more directed message. Your question or intention can be as simple as seeking guidance for the day or as specific as seeking insight into a particular challenge. Phrase your question in a way that opens the door to insight, such as, *"What should I focus on today?"* or *"What guidance does God have for me regarding this situation?"*

REFLECTING ON THE MEANING

Next, explore the meaning of the card. Consider how the themes of the story or the traits of the character might offer insight into your daily life or the specific situation you're contemplating. Ask yourself:

- **What lessons does this biblical story teach?**
- **How do these lessons apply to my current situation or mindset?**
- **What is the emotional tone of the card, and how does it reflect my own feelings?**

APPLYING THE INSIGHT

Reflection on the card's message can reveal actionable insights or shifts in perception. Perhaps the card encourages patience, suggests a need for action, or calls for introspection. Consider writing down your thoughts, the card's message, and any steps you feel inspired to take in your journal.

DAILY PRACTICE

Making the Single Card Spread a part of your daily routine can enrich your spiritual practice and personal growth journey. Over time, you will not only become more familiar with the biblical stories and symbols but also develop a deeper intuition and understanding of how these ancient wisdoms can guide your daily life.

CLOSING YOUR READING

Conclude your reading with a moment of gratitude for the guidance received. Whether you offer thanks in prayer, meditation, or a simple acknowledgment, recognizing the wisdom imparted by the Biblical Tarot deepens your connection to the divine and to your own spiritual journey.

By incorporating the Single Card Spread into your practice, you create a daily ritual of reflection, guidance, and growth, allowing the rich tapestry of biblical narratives and Tarot symbolism to illuminate your path.

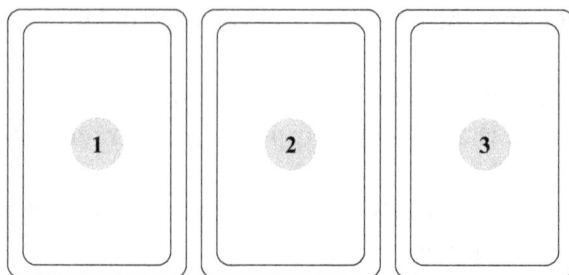

Three Card Spread

The Three Card Spread is a versatile and widely used format in tarot reading, offering insight into the past, present, and future dynamics of a situation. When applied to the Biblical Tarot, this spread not only reveals the flow of temporal events but also invites reflection on deeper spiritual lessons and biblical wisdom. Here's how to enrich your experience with the Three Card Spread:

SETTING YOUR INTENTION

As with any tarot reading, start by setting a clear intention or question. The Three Card Spread can be adapted to various inquiries, from understanding personal growth to navigating specific challenges. Your question should be open-ended, inviting deep reflection, such as, *"What lessons can I learn from my recent experience?"* or *"How can I approach my current situation for the best outcome?"*

INTERPRETING EACH POSITION

Past (Card 1): This card reflects the events, lessons, or emotional states from your past that influence your current situation. Consider the biblical story or character on the card. What lessons did they learn? How does this reflect your own past experiences or lessons learned?

Present (Card 2): The present card offers insight into your current situation or state of mind. It highlights the challenges or opportunities you are currently facing. Again, relate the biblical narrative or character depicted on the card to your own life. What wisdom does it offer for your present circumstances?

Future (Card 3): This card suggests a possible outcome or direction based on the current trajectory. The future card is not a fixed prediction but an indication of where things might head if you continue on your current path. Reflect on the biblical story or figure represented and consider the lessons or outcomes they suggest for your future.

REFLECTING ON THE SPREAD AS A WHOLE

After interpreting each card individually, step back to view the spread as an interconnected story. How do the past, present, and future cards relate to each other? Is there a continuous theme or lesson that runs through them?

APPLYING THE GUIDANCE

Consider the actionable insights or shifts in perspective the reading offers. How can the wisdom of the past card inform your understanding of the present? What steps can you take in the present, as suggested by the middle card, to navigate towards the future depicted in the right card? Writing down your reflections can help clarify these insights and guide your actions.

THREE CARD SPREAD VARIANTS

The Three Card Spread is highly adaptable and can be customized to explore a variety of themes and questions beyond the traditional "past, present, future" layout. By assigning different meanings to the three positions, you can tailor the spread to suit your specific needs or areas of inquiry. Here are several alternative ways to use the Three Card Spread with the Biblical Tarot:

1. Situation - Action - Outcome
- **Situation:** *Card 1 represents the current situation or the context of the question.*
- **Action:** *Card 2 suggests the action to take or the attitude to adopt for addressing the situation.*
- **Outcome:** *Card 3 provides insight into the possible outcome or resolution if the suggested action is taken.*

2. Mind - Body - Spirit
- **Mind (Card 1):** *This card reflects your current mental state or thoughts regarding the question.*
- **Body (Card 2):** *Represents the physical aspects or actions that are relevant to the situation.*
- **Spirit (Card 3):** *Offers insight into your spiritual state or the spiritual guidance you are receiving.*

3. Strengths - Weaknesses - Advice
- **Strengths (Card 1):** *Highlights your strengths or resources that you can leverage in your situation.*
- **Weaknesses (Card 2):** *Points out potential weaknesses or challenges to be aware of.*
- **Advice (Card 3):** *Provides guidance on how to navigate the situation, considering your strengths and weaknesses.*

4. Option 1 - Option 2 - Outcome
This spread is useful when you are facing a choice between two paths.
- **Option 1 (Card 1):** *Insights into the first option.*
- **Option 2 (Card 2):** *Insights into the second option.*
- **Outcome (Card 3):** *Provides a broader perspective on the potential outcome of choosing either option.*

5. Obstacle - Action - Help
- **Obstacle (Card 1):** *Identifies the main challenge or obstacle you are facing.*
- **Action (Card 2):** *Suggests a course of action to overcome the obstacle.*
- **Help (Card 3):** *Reveals the external forces, people, or resources that can assist you in this situation.*

6. What I Think - What I Feel - What I Do
- **What I Think (Card 1):** *Your current thoughts or beliefs about your situation.*
- **What I Feel (Card 2):** *Emotions you are experiencing.*
- **What I Do (Card 3):** *The actions you are taking or should consider taking.*

7. The Nature of Your Problem - The Cause - The Solution

- **The Nature of Your Problem (Card 1):** *Clarifies what the core issue or problem is.*
- **The Cause (Card 2):** *Explores the underlying causes or contributing factors to the problem.*
- **The Solution (Card 3):** *Offers insight into a potential solution or way to address the problem.*

8. You - The Other Person - The Relationship

This spread is ideal for understanding dynamics in a relationship.

- **You (Card 1):** *Your role or state in the relationship.*
- **The Other Person (Card 2):** *The other person's role or state.*
- **The Relationship (Card 3):** *The current state or future potential of the relationship.*

These variations of the Three Card Spread provide flexible frameworks for exploring a wide range of questions and themes with the Biblical Tarot. By adapting the spread to fit your specific inquiry, you can gain deeper insights and more actionable guidance.

CLOSING YOUR READING

End your reading with a moment of gratitude for the guidance received, whether through prayer, meditation, or a simple acknowledgment. This helps to close the session on a positive note and reinforces your connection to the spiritual wisdom the Biblical Tarot provides.

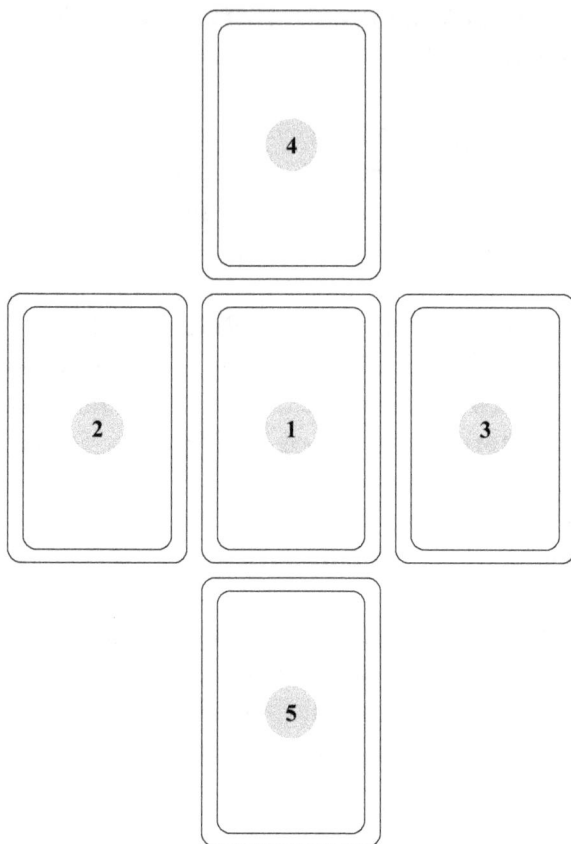

Five Card Spread

The Five Card Spread is a versatile and detailed layout that offers a nuanced view of the situation, making it an excellent choice for deeper exploration. When used with the Biblical Tarot, this spread can provide profound insights into your spiritual journey, decision-making processes, and the dynamics at play in your life. Here's how to enrich your experience with the Five Card Spread:

SETTING UP THE SPREAD

Center Card [1] (Current Situation): This card represents the present situation or the core issue at hand. It serves as the focal point of the reading, around which all other cards are interpreted.

Left Card [2] (Past Influences): Placed to the left of the center card, this card sheds light on past events, behaviors, or decisions that are influencing the current situation.

Right Card [3] (Future Influences): This card, placed to the right of the center card, signifies upcoming influences that could affect the situation. These could be challenges or opportunities that have not yet manifested.

Top Card [4] (Possible Outcome): Positioned above the center card, this card offers a glimpse into a possible future outcome, based on the current trajectory and influences.

Bottom Card [5] (Underlying Factors): Located below the center card, it reveals the underlying factors or subconscious aspects of the situation that might not be immediately apparent.

INTERPRETING THE CARDS

Begin with the center card to understand the present situation. Then, sequentially move through the cards—past influences, possible outcome, future influences, and underlying factors.

DEEPENING YOUR UNDERSTANDING

Connecting the Dots: After interpreting each card individually, look for the overarching narrative that emerges from the spread. How do the past and future influences converge on the current situation? How do the underlying factors shape the potential outcome?

Biblical Reflections: For each card, consider the biblical narrative in depth. How did the characters in these stories face their challenges? What spiritual lessons were learned? Apply these reflections to your own life circumstances.

Actionable Insights: The Five Card Spread often highlights areas of challenge and opportunity. Based on your insights, consider practical steps or spiritual practices that could address the issues revealed by the cards. This might involve seeking forgiveness, practicing gratitude, or making a courageous decision.

FIVE CARD SPREAD VARIANTS

The Five Card Spread is adaptable and can be customized for various purposes beyond traditional layouts, offering rich, multifaceted insights. Here are some innovative ways to use the Five Card Spread with the Biblical Tarot, tailored to explore different dimensions of your questions or situations:

The Cross of Insight

This layout offers a comprehensive view, focusing on how spiritual and subconscious factors interact with temporal influences.

- **Card 1 (Center):** *The core issue or question.*
- **Card 2 (Left):** *The past affecting the situation.*
- **Card 3 (Right):** *Potential future outcomes based on current paths.*
- **Card 4 (Above):** *Higher influences or spiritual guidance.*
- **Card 5 (Below):** *Subconscious influences or underlying themes.*

The Elements of Life

Each card corresponds to a different aspect of your life, providing a holistic overview of your situation.

- **Card 1 (Soul):** *Your current spiritual state or spiritual advice.*
- **Card 2 (Water):** *Emotional influences or relationships.*
- **Card 3 (Fire):** *Ambitions, motivations, or conflicts.*
- **Card 4 (Air):** *Thoughts, beliefs, or communication issues.*
- **Card 5 (Earth):** *Material circumstances or practical advice.*

Inner Self and Outer World

This spread is particularly useful for personal growth and understanding the dynamics of interpersonal relationships.

- **Card 1 (Self Perception):** *How you see yourself in the context of the situation.*
- **Card 2 (Others' Perception):** *How others perceive you or the role they play.*
- **Card 3 (Hopes and Fears):** *Your hopes and fears related to the issue.*
- **Card 4 (Known Challenges):** *Obstacles you are aware of.*
- **Card 5 (Unknown Factors):** *Hidden influences or outcomes you haven't considered.*

The Path Forward

Designed to offer guidance on moving forward in life, focusing on change and progression.

- **Card 1 (Current Position):** *Where you are now in your journey.*
- **Card 2 (What to Leave Behind):** *Habits, influences, or attitudes to let go of.*
- **Card 3 (What to Embrace):** *New attitudes, influences, or approaches to adopt.*
- **Card 4 (Potential Challenges):** *Challenges you might face on this path.*
- **Card 5 (Potential Outcomes):** *The possible result of following this path.*

Decision Making

This layout is helpful when faced with a choice, providing clarity on potential paths.

- **Card 1 (Situation Overview):** *An overview of the decision to be made.*
- **Card 2 (Option A):** *Insights or outcomes related to the first option.*

- **Card 3 (Option B):** *Insights or outcomes related to the second option.*
- **Card 4 (What Helps):** *Resources or factors that could aid in making the decision.*
- **Card 5 (What Hinders):** *Obstacles or challenges in making a choice.*

Conflict Resolution

Ideal for navigating personal or professional conflicts, promoting understanding and resolution.

- **Card 1 (Nature of the Conflict):** *The core issue or conflict.*
- **Card 2 (Your Perspective):** *Your stance or feelings about the conflict.*
- **Card 3 (The Other's Perspective):** *The other party's stance or feelings.*
- **Card 4 (Resolution Path):** *Possible ways to resolve or address the conflict.*
- **Card 5 (Outcome):** *The potential outcome of following the resolution path.*

WRAPPING UP THE READING

Conclude your session with a moment of gratitude for the insights received. Reflect on how the biblical wisdom embodied in the cards can guide you in navigating your situation. Consider documenting your reading and reflections in a journal to track your spiritual growth and insights over time.

The Five Card Spread, with its rich potential for deep reflection and guidance, is a powerful tool in the Biblical Tarot for exploring the complex facets of your life's journey and spiritual path.

CHAPTER 4

Major Arcana

The Major Arcana of the Biblical Tarot stands as a pillar of spiritual and archetypal wisdom, weaving the rich tapestry of biblical narratives into the timeless journey of the soul depicted in traditional Tarot. Each of the 22 cards represents a significant leap forward in the spiritual journey, guiding us through the trials, tribulations, and triumphs that define the human experience. This chapter explores the profound connection between these universal archetypes and their biblical counterparts, offering a path to deeper understanding and reflection.

THE SPIRITUAL JOURNEY

The Major Arcana can be seen as mapping out a spiritual journey, one that parallels the journey of faith and discovery found in the Bible. Starting with "The Soul" (representing innocence and the beginning of a spiritual quest) and culminating with "The World" (symbolizing completion, fulfillment, and unity with the Divine), each card marks a step on the path toward spiritual enlightenment and understanding. This journey mirrors the biblical narrative of creation, fall, redemption, and restoration, inviting reflection on personal growth, challenges, and transformations.

The Major Arcana of the Biblical Tarot offers a rich and complex layer of spiritual exploration, bridging the ancient wisdom of the Tarot with the timeless narratives of the Bible. It invites users to embark on a journey of self-discovery, reflection, and deeper understanding, illuminated by the light of biblical stories and spiritual archetypes.

The Soul

CREATION OF A LIVING BEING

*Then the LORD God formed man from the dust of the ground
and breathed the breath of life into his nostrils,
and the man became a living being.*
Genesis 2:7 BSB

THE SOUL
CREATION OF A LIVING BEING

The concept of "The Soul" as the initial creation of a living being reflects this card's themes of beginnings and untapped potential. In the biblical narrative, the soul's creation marks the start of humanity's journey, imbued with divine breath and the freedom to choose its path. This moment of creation represents purity, innocence, and the nascent stage of spiritual and existential exploration, akin to the stepping out into the unknown.

UPRIGHT KEYWORDS:	REVERSED KEYWORDS:
Beginnings	*Naivety*
Innocence	*Recklessness*
Potential	*Ignored Intuition*
Adventure	*Missed Opportunities*
Faith	

CARD MEANING IN UPRIGHT POSITION:

Symbolizes the start of a spiritual or life journey, embodying optimism, openness, and the willingness to embrace the unknown. It reflects a leap of faith and the potential for growth and discovery.

- **New Beginnings:** *Embarking on a new phase or adventure with optimism.*
- **Innocence and Purity:** *Approaching life with a clean slate, free from biases.*
- **Potential and Possibilities:** *The Soul's capacity for growth and exploration.*
- **Faith in the Journey:** *Trusting in the path ahead, even without seeing it.*

CARD MEANING IN REVERSED POSITION:

Suggests a cautionary tale of the Soul's journey, highlighting the risks of naivety, recklessness, and the failure to heed warnings or learn from experiences. It represents missed opportunities due to fear or indecision.

- **Naivety:** *Failing to see the risks or consequences of actions.*
- **Recklessness:** *Taking unnecessary risks without proper consideration.*
- **Ignored Intuition:** *Not listening to inner guidance or warnings.*
- **Missed Opportunities:** *Letting fear or indecision prevent progress.*

"The Soul" card underscores the dual nature of beginnings: the purity and hope of a new journey, alongside the potential pitfalls of innocence and naivety. It invites reflection on the soul's journey through life, emphasizing the importance of faith and learning in navigating the path from creation to fulfillment.

The Magician

MOSES

Then Moses stretched out his hand over the sea, and all that night the LORD drove back the sea with a strong east wind that turned it into dry land. So the waters were divided
Exodus 14:21 BSB

THE MAGICIAN
MOSES

Moses is a central figure in the Bible, renowned for leading the Israelites out of Egyptian bondage and towards the Promised Land. His life story is one of transformation, from a humble beginning to becoming a great leader and intermediary between God and the Israelites. Moses's act of splitting the sea represents the pinnacle of his faith and divine empowerment, making him an embodiment of The Magician's ability to harness resources and will to create miracles.

UPRIGHT KEYWORDS:	REVERSED KEYWORDS:
Manifestation	*Manipulation*
Resourcefulness	*Unutilized talents*
Power	*Poor planning*
Inspired action	*Latent potential*

CARD MEANING IN UPRIGHT POSITION:

Mastery of skills and the utilization of one's abilities and resources to achieve goals. It represents the alignment of will, desire, and the external world to bring about tangible results.

- **Manifestation:** *Utilizing skills and resources to achieve goals.*
- **Resourcefulness:** *Creative problem-solving and making the most of one's environment.*
- **Power:** *Exercising willpower and authority to direct outcomes.*
- **Inspired Action:** *Taking decisive steps with confidence and faith.*

CARD MEANING IN REVERSED POSITION:

Potential that is not being fully realized or misused. It suggests a disconnection between one's intentions and actions, leading to manipulation or wasted talent.

- **Manipulation:** *Using skills for selfish or harmful ends.*
- **Unutilized Talents:** *Having abilities that are not being employed effectively.*
- **Poor Planning:** *A lack of direction or misuse of resources.*
- **Latent Potential:** *Possessing great promise that is yet to be realized or acted upon.*

Through the story of Moses, "The Magician" card is a symbol of divine intervention and the human capacity to work in harmony with greater forces to manifest change. It highlights the balance between faith, will, and action, underscoring the potential within us to achieve seemingly impossible feats when aligned with a higher purpose.

The High Priestess

MARY MAGDALENE

Early on the first day of the week, after Jesus had risen,
He appeared first to Mary Magdalene,
from whom He had driven out seven demons.
Mark 16:9 BSB

THE HIGH PRIESTESS
MARY MAGDALENE

Mary Magdalene is a significant figure in the New Testament, often depicted as a close follower of Jesus. Seven demons had been driven out of her, and this is why shy is portrayed with seven skulls below her on the card. Seven refers symbolically to "completeness" – the total cure of all evil. Her story is a testament to personal transformation and redemption. Mary Magdalene's journey from darkness to being a witness to the resurrection embodies the themes of accessing deep, inner knowledge and the balance between seen and unseen worlds.

UPRIGHT KEYWORDS:	REVERSED KEYWORDS:
Intuition	*Secrets*
Mystery	*Disconnected from intuition*
Understanding	*Surface-level understanding*
Spiritual insight	*Hidden agendas*
Inner wisdom	

CARD MEANING IN UPRIGHT POSITION:

Deep connection to one's inner voice and intuition, suggesting a phase of introspection and understanding hidden truths. It embodies wisdom, insight, and the uncovering of mysteries.

- **Intuition:** *Trusting in one's inner guidance and insights.*
- **Mystery:** *Embracing the unknown and seeking deeper understanding.*
- **Understanding:** *Achieving clarity and awareness beyond the obvious.*
- **Spiritual Insight:** *Accessing hidden knowledge and truths.*

CARD MEANING IN REVERSED POSITION:

Indicates a disconnection from inner wisdom, leading to confusion, ignoring one's intuition, or being misled by superficial appearances. It suggests secrets or truths that are not yet revealed or acknowledged.

- **Secrets:** *Keeping or being kept from important information.*
- **Disconnected Intuition:** *Ignoring inner guidance, leading to poor decisions.*
- **Surface-level Understanding:** *Overlooking deeper meanings and truths.*
- **Hidden Agendas:** *Unrevealed motives or misunderstandings.*

The "High Priestess" card is a symbol of profound personal transformation, highlighting the journey from inner turmoil to enlightenment. It underscores the card's association with intuition, the subconscious, and the revelation of truths, emphasizing the power of inner wisdom and spiritual insight in navigating life's challenges.

The Empress

MARY, MOTHER OF JESUS

*The angel replied, "The Holy Spirit will come upon you,
and the power of the Most High will overshadow you.
So the Holy One to be born will be called the Son of God.*
Luke 1:35 BSB

THE EMPRESS
MARY, MOTHER OF JESUS

Mary, the mother of Jesus, is a central figure in Christianity, revered for her obedience, faith, and role in the divine plan of salvation. Her acceptance of her role, despite the challenges, exemplifies unconditional love, nurturing, and the birthing of new ideas and spiritual paths. Mary's journey embodies the essence of The Empress, representing fertility, creativity, and the nurturing of life and faith.

UPRIGHT KEYWORDS:	REVERSED KEYWORDS:
Fertility	*Neglect*
Motherhood	*Overprotectiveness*
Creation	*Lack of growth*
Nature	*Stifled creativity*
Abundance	

CARD MEANING IN UPRIGHT POSITION:

Celebration of fertility, creativity, and the nurturing aspects of life. It embodies abundance, growth, and the loving care that fosters the flourishing of all things.

- **Fertility:** *The potential for new life, ideas, or opportunities.*
- **Motherhood:** *The nurturing and loving care that encourages growth.*
- **Creation:** *The birthing of new projects, relationships, or spiritual paths.*
- **Nature:** *A connection to the natural world and its cycles of growth.*
- **Abundance:** *A period of plentifulness and satisfaction.*

CARD MEANING IN REVERSED POSITION:

Suggests potential issues in the nurturing process, such as neglect, overprotectiveness, or the stifling of growth and creativity. It indicates a need to reassess how care and abundance are being applied or withheld.

- **Neglect:** *Failing to provide the necessary care or attention.*
- **Overprotectiveness:** *Smothering or restricting growth out of fear.*
- **Lack of Growth:** *Stagnation or the absence of development and progress.*
- **Stifled Creativity:** *The suppression of new ideas or expressions.*

Through the story of Mary, mother of Jesus, "The Empress" tarot card is reimagined as a powerful symbol of divine femininity, embodying the principles of creation, nurturing, and the unconditional love that fosters all life. It emphasizes the importance of care, abundance, and the nurturing spirit that leads to growth and fulfillment.

The Emperor

KING SOLOMON

...behold, I will do what you have asked. I will give you a wise and discerning heart, so that there will never have been another like you, nor will there ever be.
1 Kings 3:12 BSB

THE EMPEROR
KING SOLOMON

King Solomon, son of David and Bathsheba, was the third king of Israel. His reign is often considered Israel's golden age, marked by peace, prosperity, and architectural achievements, including the building of the First Temple in Jerusalem. Solomon is most renowned for his wisdom, granted by God in response to his prayer for an understanding heart to judge his people fairly. His story encapsulates the balance of power, wisdom, and justice, embodying The Emperor's essence.

UPRIGHT KEYWORDS:	REVERSED KEYWORDS:
Authority	*Tyranny*
Stability	*Rigidity*
Leadership	*Loss of control*
Wisdom	*Authoritarianism*
Structure	*Lack of discipline*

CARD MEANING IN UPRIGHT POSITION:

Strong leadership, authority, and the establishment of law and order. It signifies the ability to make decisions based on wisdom and to provide stability and structure.

- **Authority:** *Commanding respect and exercising rightful power.*
- **Stability:** *Providing a secure and stable environment.*
- **Leadership:** *Guiding others with wisdom and fairness.*
- **Wisdom:** *Making decisions informed by insight and experience.*
- **Structure:** *Establishing laws, rules, and order for collective well-being.*

CARD MEANING IN REVERSED POSITION:

Indicates abuse of power, authoritarianism, or a lack of discipline. It may represent a leader who is rigid, tyrannical, or unable to adapt, leading to chaos rather than order.

- **Tyranny:** *Misusing power and controlling others oppressively.*
- **Rigidity:** *Being inflexible, which may hinder progress.*
- **Loss of Control:** *The inability to maintain authority or order.*
- **Authoritarianism:** *Leading with a lack of regard for others' autonomy.*
- **Lack of Discipline:** *Failing to apply self-control or to structure effectively.*

"The Emperor" tarot card is a symbol of enlightened leadership, emphasizing the balance between authority and wisdom. It invites reflection on the principles of leadership, authority, and the ethical responsibilities that come with power.

The High Priest

AARON, BROTHER OF MOSES

"...You must distinguish between the holy and the common, between the clean and the unclean, so that you may teach the Israelites all the statutes that the LORD has given them through Moses."
Leviticus 10:10-11 BSB

THE HIGH PRIEST
AARON BROTHER OF MOSES

Aaron, as Moses' brother and the first high priest of Israel, played a critical role in the establishment and maintenance of the Israelite's religious practices and traditions. He was a key figure in communicating God's laws and performing sacred rituals, embodying the qualities of spiritual leadership, guidance, and tradition. Aaron's life illustrates the complexities of adhering to divine will while facing the challenges of leadership and faith.

UPRIGHT KEYWORDS:	REVERSED KEYWORDS:
Tradition	*Rebellion*
Spiritual authority	*Independence*
Conformity	*Challenging traditions*
Mentorship	*Unconventional wisdom*
Wisdom	*Dogmatism*

CARD MEANING IN UPRIGHT POSITION:

Respect for tradition and established beliefs. It suggests guidance, spiritual authority, and the importance of communal rituals and ceremonies. This stance encourages learning from the past and adhering to established spiritual or moral laws.

- **Tradition and Conformity:** *Adherence to established beliefs and practices.*
- **Spiritual Authority:** *Guidance from or role as a mentor within a traditional framework.*
- **Communal Beliefs:** *Emphasis on community and shared spiritual practices.*
- **Educational Guidance:** *Learning or teaching within established doctrines.*

CARD MEANING IN REVERSED POSITION:

Signifies a questioning of traditional values and norms. It encourages independence in spiritual matters, challenging established paths, and seeking personal truths outside conventional systems. This aspect of the card reflects the journey of finding one's own spiritual authority.

- **Questioning Traditions:** *Challenging or rejecting conventional beliefs.*
- **Spiritual Independence:** *Seeking personal paths outside traditional frameworks.*
- **Rejection of Authority:** *Resistance to traditional spiritual or moral leaders.*
- **Innovation in Belief:** *Exploring new or unconventional spiritual ideas.*

Aaron's portrayal as the High Priest bridges the divine and the human, offering a complex view of spiritual authority that is rooted in tradition but not immune to the challenges of leadership and personal faith. His story invites reflection on the balance between following established paths and forging one's own way in spiritual matters.

The Lovers

ADAM AND EVE

And Adam named his wife Eve,
because she would be the mother of all the living.
Genesis 3:20 BSB

Adam and Eve, according to the Bible, were the first humans created by God and placed in the Garden of Eden. Their story is foundational, illustrating themes of love, choice, temptation, and the consequences of their actions. Their decision to eat from the Tree of Knowledge, leading to their expulsion from Eden, highlights the complexities of free will, temptation, and the pursuit of wisdom at the cost of harmony.

THE LOVERS
ADAM AND EVE

UPRIGHT KEYWORDS:	REVERSED KEYWORDS:
Unity	*Disharmony*
Love	*Imbalance*
Harmony	*Conflict*
Choices	*Disconnection*
Moral decisions	*Poor choices*

CARD MEANING IN UPRIGHT POSITION:

Represents a harmonious relationship, the importance of mutual choices, and the alignment of values and ethics. It signifies love, connection, and the critical decisions that shape our lives.

- **Unity and Harmony:** *The joining of two entities in love or agreement.*
- **Choices:** *Critical decisions that affect the course of life or relationships.*
- **Moral Decisions:** *The ethical dilemmas that test values and integrity.*
- **Alignment of Values:** *Shared beliefs and ethics that strengthen bonds.*
- **Love:** *A deep, spiritual or emotional connection between individuals.*

CARD MEANING IN REVERSED POSITION:

Indicates disharmony, misalignment, and the consequences of poor decisions within a relationship. It suggests conflict, loss of balance, and the challenges of disconnection or miscommunication.

- **Disharmony:** *A lack of understanding or agreement, leading to conflict.*
- **Imbalance:** *Unequal or unilateral decisions affecting a relationship.*
- **Conflict:** *Disputes and disagreements arising from misaligned values.*
- **Disconnection:** *Emotional or physical separation from a partner or loved ones.*
- **Poor Choices:** *Decisions made without consideration of consequences or ethics.*

"The Lovers" card is a powerful narrative of love, choice, and the consequences that those choices bring to relationships. It offers profound insights into the dynamics of relationships, and the enduring consequences of actions driven by desire and curiosity.

The Chariot

PHARAOH'S PURSUIT

*And the Egyptians chased after them – all Pharaoh's horses, chariots,
and horsemen – and followed them into the sea.*
Exodus 14:23 BSB

In the context of the Exodus story, Pharaoh represents the epitome of earthly power and opposition to the will of God, as manifested through Moses and the Israelites' quest for freedom. His decision to pursue the Israelites with chariots symbolizes a direct confrontation with divine will, embodying the struggle between control and surrender.

THE CHARIOT
PHARAOH'S PURSUIT

UPRIGHT KEYWORDS:	REVERSED KEYWORDS:
Willpower	*Lack of control*
Victory	*Aggression*
Control	*Obstacles*
Determination	*Recklessness*
Overcoming obstacles	*Defeat*

CARD MEANING IN UPRIGHT POSITION:

Victory achieved through determination and control. It represents the ability to navigate challenges with confidence and to direct one's path toward achievement.

- **Willpower:** *Harnessing inner strength to pursue goals.*
- **Victory:** *Achieving success through determination and effort.*
- **Control:** *Directing one's path and overcoming external challenges.*
- **Determination:** *Persisting against opposition to reach objectives.*
- **Overcoming Obstacles:** *Navigating difficulties with confidence and strategy.*

CARD MEANING IN REVERSED POSITION:

Implies a scenario where control is lost, leading to aggression or defeat. It suggests being overwhelmed by obstacles or engaging in a battle that cannot be won by force alone.

- **Lack of Control:** *Being overwhelmed by external forces or emotions.*
- **Aggression:** *Using force inappropriately, leading to negative consequences.*
- **Obstacles:** *Facing challenges that hinder progress.*
- **Recklessness:** *Acting without foresight, risking unnecessary conflict.*
- **Defeat:** *Failing to overcome challenges, often due to misdirected effort.*

"The Chariot" card reflects a narrative of conflict and the quest for freedom, emphasizing the dual nature of determination: the power to overcome challenges and the potential downfall of unchecked aggression. This story highlights the importance of balanced control and the recognition of when to push forward and when to let go.

Strength

DANIEL IN THE LION'S DEN

"...My God sent His angel and shut the mouths of the lions. They have not hurt me, for I was found innocent in His sight, and I have done no wrong against you, O king."
Daniel 6:22 BSB

Daniel, a Jewish prophet, blessed by God with the wisdom and ability to interpret dreams, is known for his unwavering faith, even when faced with death. His story illustrates his moral and spiritual strength. Despite being thrown into the den as punishment for praying to God (against the king's decree), Daniel's faith protected him, and he emerged unscathed. His integrity and trust in divine power make him a perfect embodiment of the Strength card's themes.

UPRIGHT KEYWORDS:	REVERSED KEYWORDS:
Inner strength	*Self-doubt*
Courage	*Weakness*
Patience	*Lack of faith*
Compassion	*Loss of control*
Moral integrity	*Impatience*

CARD MEANING IN UPRIGHT POSITION:

Represents the power of inner strength, courage, and conviction. It signifies overcoming challenges through faith, patience, and compassion, rather than through force.

- **Inner Strength:** *Drawing on deep moral and spiritual reserves to face challenges.*
- **Courage:** *Facing fear with conviction and calmness.*
- **Patience:** *Trusting in the process and timing, despite challenges.*
- **Compassion:** *Approaching situations with understanding and gentleness.*
- **Moral Integrity:** *Staying true to one's principles and beliefs.*

CARD MEANING IN REVERSED POSITION:

Self-doubt, fear, and loss of faith. It reveals a struggle to maintain inner strength or control, leading to impatience and potentially making decisions out of weakness.

- **Self-doubt:** *Questioning one's ability to overcome obstacles.*
- **Weakness:** *Feeling unable to assert one's inner strength effectively.*
- **Lack of Faith:** *Losing sight of spiritual conviction or moral compass.*
- **Loss of Control:** *Being overwhelmed by circumstances or emotions.*
- **Impatience:** *Forcing issues rather than allowing them to unfold naturally.*

The "Strength" tarot card is a powerful testament to the power of faith and integrity. Daniel's experience illuminates the true nature of strength: not as physical power, but as the courage to stand firm in one's beliefs and to face adversity with grace and trust in a higher power.

The Hermit

JOHN THE BAPTIST

This is he who was spoken of through the prophet Isaiah:
"A voice of one calling in the wilderness,
'Prepare the way for the Lord,
make straight paths for Him.'"
Matthew 3:3 BSB

John the Baptist is a pivotal figure in the New Testament, known for his ascetic lifestyle in the wilderness and his role in baptizing Jesus. His life was marked by deep spiritual commitment, reflection, and the calling to prepare others for the coming of the Messiah.

John's dedication to his faith, despite societal detachment, embodies the themes of seeking wisdom in solitude and guiding others on their spiritual journey.

UPRIGHT KEYWORDS:	REVERSED KEYWORDS:
Introspection	*Isolation*
Guidance	*Loneliness*
Solitude	*Withdrawn*
Contemplation	*Ignored guidance*
Inner wisdom	*Inward focus*

CARD MEANING IN UPRIGHT POSITION:

Pursuit of deeper truth through solitude and introspection. It signifies a period of self-discovery, spiritual enlightenment, and the sharing of acquired wisdom.

- **Introspection:** *Engaging in self-reflection to understand deeper truths.*
- **Guidance:** *Offering wisdom and guidance based on personal insights.*
- **Solitude:** *Finding peace and clarity in solitude.*
- **Contemplation:** *Considering spiritual or philosophical concepts deeply.*
- **Inner Wisdom:** *Accessing and trusting one's inner wisdom.*

CARD MEANING IN REVERSED POSITION:

Excessive isolation or loneliness, a disconnection from society, or the refusal to heed or share inner wisdom. It suggests a need to reconnect with the world or others.

- **Isolation:** *Feeling cut off from others or society.*
- **Loneliness:** *Experiencing the negative aspects of solitude.*
- **Withdrawn:** *Pulling away from the world to an unhealthy degree.*
- **Ignored Guidance:** *Failing to heed one's own insights or advice.*
- **Inward Focus:** *Becoming too absorbed in one's own world, neglecting the external.*

"The Hermit" card is a symbol of spiritual awakening, introspection, and the importance of solitude in finding one's path. John's life exemplifies the journey toward inner enlightenment and the imperative to share that light with others, underscoring the balance between solitude and societal engagement in spiritual growth.

Wheel Within a Wheel

CYCLES OF LIFE

For everything there is a season,
and a time for every purpose under heaven
Ecclesiastes 3:1 BSB

This card doesn't focus on a single character, but rather on the universal experience shared by all of humanity as depicted in the Bible. It acknowledges the seasons of life, the rise and fall of nations, and the personal journeys of faith, hardship, and redemption. It depicts the cyclical nature of human experiences, the inevitability of change, and the guiding hand of destiny or divine will

This theme reflects the ongoing dance of creation and renewal echoed throughout the Bible.

UPRIGHT KEYWORDS:	REVERSED KEYWORDS:
Cycles	*Resistance to change*
Change	*Bad luck*
Destiny	*Breaking cycles*
Good fortune	*Stagnation*
Turning points	

CARD MEANING IN UPRIGHT POSITION:

Represents acceptance of the cycles of life and the positive changes they bring. It signifies being in alignment with destiny and recognizing the opportunities that come with life's ups and downs.

- **Cycles:** *Awareness of life's natural cycles and rhythms.*
- **Change:** *Embracing change as an opportunity for growth.*
- **Destiny:** *Trusting in the unfolding of one's destined path.*
- **Good Fortune:** *Being at a high point or experiencing a positive turn.*
- **Turning Points:** *Recognizing and seizing the critical junctures in life.*

CARD MEANING IN REVERSED POSITION:

Struggle against the natural flow of life, resistance to change, or experiencing a run of bad luck. It suggests a need to break free from negative cycles or to reassess one's approach to life's inevitable changes.

- **Resistance to Change:** *Struggling against the natural flow of life.*
- **Bad Luck:** *Experiencing a series of unfortunate events or a low point.*
- **Breaking Cycles:** *The need to break free from negative patterns.*
- **Stagnation:** *Feeling stuck or immobilized by fear of change.*

"The Wheel Within a Wheel" tarot card is a reflection of the biblical understanding of time, change, and divine guidance. This perspective emphasizes the importance of embracing life's cyclical nature, recognizing that each phase brings its own challenges and blessings, and understanding that faith and acceptance can guide one through the ups and downs of existence.

Justice

THE TEN COMMANDMENTS

You must walk in all the ways that the LORD your God has commanded you, so that you may live and prosper and prolong your days in the land that you will possess.
Deuteronomy 5:33 BSB

JUSTICE
THE TEN COMMANDMENTS

The Ten Commandments were given to Moses by God on Mount Sinai and represent God's laws for His people, Israel. They encompass duties to God and to fellow humans, laying down a framework for justice, respect, and ethical conduct.

The commandments are fundamental to the Judeo-Christian moral and legal systems, symbolizing the divine origin of justice and the importance of living in accordance with divine and moral law.

UPRIGHT KEYWORDS:	REVERSED KEYWORDS:
Fairness	Injustice
Truth	Bias
Law	Dishonesty
Accountability	Avoidance of accountability
Moral integrity	Unfairness

CARD MEANING IN UPRIGHT POSITION:

Depicts a clear understanding of right and wrong, the importance of fairness, and the need for accountability. It signifies making decisions or judgments that are balanced, ethical, and just.

- **Fairness:** *Acting with impartiality and integrity.*
- **Truth:** *Seeking the truth and being honest in one's dealings.*
- **Law:** *Upholding and respecting legal and moral codes.*
- **Accountability:** *Taking responsibility for one's actions.*
- **Moral Integrity:** *Living in alignment with ethical principles.*

CARD MEANING IN REVERSED POSITION:

Points to a situation where justice is not being served, where decisions are biased or unfair, or where one may be avoiding accountability for their actions. It suggests a misalignment with ethical or moral principles.

- **Injustice:** *Experiencing or contributing to unfair treatment.*
- **Bias:** *Allowing personal prejudices to influence decisions.*
- **Dishonesty:** *Being untruthful or misleading in one's actions.*
- **Avoidance of Accountability:** *Shunning responsibility for one's actions.*
- **Unfairness:** *Engaging in or being the victim of biased judgments.*

"The Justice" tarot card is a profound reflection on the principles of divine and moral law, emphasizing the importance of living in alignment with these laws for the betterment of oneself and society. It underscores the card's themes of accountability, fairness, and the necessity of making ethical decisions grounded in truth and integrity.

The Hanged Man

PETER'S CRUCIFIXION

Then Jesus said to all of them,
"If anyone wants to come after Me, he must deny himself and take
up his cross daily and follow Me. For whoever wants to save his life
will lose it, but whoever loses his life for My sake will save it.
Luke 9:23-24 BSB

THE HANGED MAN
PETER'S CRUCIFIXION

Peter, one of Jesus' closest disciples, is a foundational figure in Christianity. Known for his bold faith and, at times, his impetuousness, Peter's journey with Jesus includes moments of profound insight and human frailty. His eventual martyrdom, according to tradition, symbolizes ultimate faithfulness and humility, choosing to be crucified upside down because he did not see himself as equal to Jesus. Peter's story is a testament to personal transformation and the power of faith.

UPRIGHT KEYWORDS:	REVERSED KEYWORDS:
Sacrifice	*Stagnation*
Release	*Unwillingness to sacrifice*
Perspective shift	*Missed opportunities for*
Surrender	*growth*
New insights	*Fear of letting go*

CARD MEANING IN UPRIGHT POSITION:

Embracing sacrifice or surrender for a higher purpose, the willingness to see things from a new perspective, and the acceptance of necessary change.

- **Sacrifice:** *Embracing personal loss for greater gain or understanding.*
- **Release:** *Letting go of what no longer serves to make way for the new.*
- **Perspective Shift:** *Viewing life or challenges from a new angle.*
- **Surrender:** *Accepting what cannot be changed and focusing on what can be learned.*
- **New Insights:** *Gaining wisdom and understanding through trials.*

CARD MEANING IN REVERSED POSITION:

Resistance to change, fear of sacrifice, missing the opportunity for growth, and clinging to outdated perspectives or ego.

- **Stagnation:** *Refusing to move forward or change despite knowing it's necessary.*
- **Unwillingness to Sacrifice:** *Holding back from making needed changes due to fear or ego.*
- **Missed Opportunities for Growth:** *Ignoring the chance to evolve spiritually or emotionally.*
- **Fear of Letting Go:** *Clinging to control or the familiar at the cost of development..*

Through the story of Peter's crucifixion, "The Hanged Man" card is a display of profound faith, humility, and the transformative power of viewing one's life and sacrifices from a new perspective. Peter's ultimate act of humility and devotion highlights the themes of surrender, sacrifice, and the wisdom that comes from releasing the ego in favor of spiritual growth and deeper understanding.

Death

THE FOURTH HORSEMAN

And behold, a pale horse,
and the name of he who sat on it was Death.
Revelation 6:8 WEB

The fourth horseman of the apocalypse, as described in the Book of Revelation, is a symbolic figure representing death and the profound changes that follow in its wake. Accompanied by Hades, the horseman is granted power to bring about death through various means, symbolizing the inevitable and transformative nature of end times. This character underscores the theme of inevitable change and the cycle of life and death.

UPRIGHT KEYWORDS:	REVERSED KEYWORDS:
Endings	*Resistance to change*
Transformation, transition	*Fear of loss*
Letting go	*Stagnation*
Rebirth	*Unfinished business*

CARD MEANING IN UPRIGHT POSITION:

Acceptance of change and the understanding that endings are necessary for new beginnings. It represents the natural cycle of transformation that leads to renewal and growth.

- **Endings:** *Acknowledging the conclusion of a phase or aspect of life.*
- **Transformation:** *Undergoing significant change, leading to new perspectives.*
- **Transition:** *Moving from one state of being to another, embracing evolution.*
- **Letting Go:** *Releasing what no longer serves to make way for new growth.*
- **Rebirth:** *The emergence of new opportunities and beginnings after an ending.*

CARD MEANING IN REVERSED POSITION:

Struggle against the natural flow of life, a reluctance to accept change, and the fear of letting go. It shows stagnation, clinging to the past, or the refusal to move forward.

- **Resistance to Change:** *Holding on to the past or current situations out of fear.*
- **Fear of Loss:** *Worrying about the implications of letting go or changing.*
- **Stagnation:** *Remaining stuck due to reluctance to progress or evolve.*
- **Unfinished Business:** *Incomplete closure that hinders moving forward.*

"The Death" card is a potent symbol of the transformative power of endings. It illustrates the necessary cycle of death and rebirth, urging an embrace of change as a pathway to renewal and growth. It serves as a reminder of the natural progression of life and the potential for new beginnings that arise from the ashes of the old.

Temperance

MARY AND MARTHA

Jesus answered her,
"Martha, Martha, you are anxious and troubled about many things,
but one thing is needed. Mary has chosen the good part,
which will not be taken away from her."
Luke 10:41-42 WEB

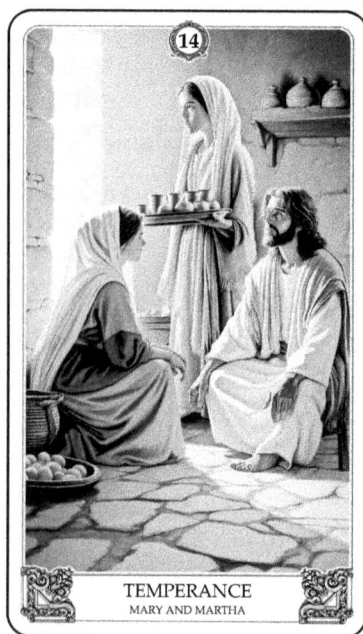

TEMPERANCE
MARY AND MARTHA

Mary and Martha, sisters of Lazarus, offer contrasting approaches to Jesus' visit. Martha is preoccupied with the hospitality duties, stressing over the details of serving their guest, while Mary chooses to sit at Jesus' feet, listening to his teachings. This story contrasts the active service and spiritual attentiveness, embodying the Temperance card's call for balance between worldly responsibilities and spiritual well-being.

UPRIGHT KEYWORDS:	REVERSED KEYWORDS:
Balance	Imbalance
Moderation	Excess
Patience	Lack of vision
Purpose	Discord
Harmony	Extremes

CARD MEANING IN UPRIGHT POSITION:

Signifies the importance of creating balance and harmony in life, blending spiritual practices with daily responsibilities. It encourages moderation and finding a middle path that respects both action and contemplation.

- **Balance:** *Achieving equilibrium in various aspects of life.*
- **Moderation:** *Avoiding extremes and finding the middle way.*
- **Patience:** *Practicing patience and understanding timing.*
- **Purpose:** *Aligning actions with deeper spiritual values.*
- **Harmony:** *Fostering inner and outer harmony through balanced choices.*

CARD MEANING IN REVERSED POSITION:

Implies a life thrown out of balance by excessive focus on either physical tasks or spiritual pursuits to the neglect of the other. It suggests a need to realign priorities and rediscover equilibrium.

- **Imbalance:** *Living in disharmony due to neglecting certain areas of life.*
- **Excess:** *Going to extremes in behavior, work, or spirituality.*
- **Lack of Vision:** *Missing the bigger picture due to focus on minutiae.*
- **Discord:** *Experiencing inner unrest from lack of balance.*
- **Extremes:** *Swinging between extremes without finding a stable center.*

"The Temperance" card is all about the wisdom of choosing the "better part"—the balance between being and doing, listening and acting, spirituality and daily life. It invites reflection on how to integrate spiritual well-being with worldly responsibilities, highlighting the journey toward a harmonious and moderated life.

The Devil

SATAN TEMPTING HUMANS TO SIN

But each one is tempted when by his own evil desires he is lured away and enticed. Then after desire has conceived, it gives birth to sin; and sin, when it is full-grown, gives birth to death.
James 1:14-15 BSB

THE DEVIL
SATAN TEMPTING HUMANS TO SIN

Satan, often depicted as a fallen angel, embodies the ultimate tempter or adversary in Christian theology. He is known for his cunning ability to deceive, seduce, and lead humans away from divine will, enticing them into actions that bind them to the material world or their own shadows, away from spiritual truth.

UPRIGHT KEYWORDS:	REVERSED KEYWORDS:
Bondage	*Liberation*
Materialism	*Understanding*
Temptation	*Reclaiming power*
Ignorance enslavement	*Awakening*

CARD MEANING IN UPRIGHT POSITION:

Symbolizes the aspects of our lives where we find ourselves bound by our desires, fears, or ignorance. It represents the chains we place on ourselves by giving in to temptations that lead us away from our true path.

- **Bondage:** *Being trapped by one's own choices or desires.*
- **Materialism:** *Focusing solely on the material at the expense of the spiritual.*
- **Temptation:** *The allure of the forbidden or easy path.*
- **Ignorance:** *Lack of awareness or understanding of one's own entrapment.*
- **Enslavement:** *Giving up freedom for an illusion of security or pleasure.*

CARD MEANING IN REVERSED POSITION:

Awakening and liberation from the chains that bind us. It signifies recognizing the illusions of our fears and desires and taking steps to break free from the things that hold us back.

- **Liberation:** *Breaking free from self-imposed chains.*
- **Understanding:** *Gaining insight into one's situation and the illusions that bind.*
- **Reclaiming Power:** *Taking back control over one's life and decisions.*
- **Awakening:** *The realization that leads to spiritual or personal freedom.*
-

"The Devil" card is a narrative of the constant human struggle with temptation, materialism, and the pursuit of superficial desires at the expense of spiritual growth. It calls for reflection on the nature of our chains and the importance of conscious choice in seeking liberation and true freedom.

The Tower

TOWER OF BABEL

"Come," they said, "let us build for ourselves a city with a tower that reaches to the heavens, that we may make a name for ourselves and not be scattered over the face of all the earth."
Genesis 11:4 BSB

The Tower of Babel story from Genesis describes humanity's united effort to build a tower tall enough to reach heaven. This act of pride and ambition led God to confuse their language, making them unable to communicate and cooperate, which resulted in the scattering of people across the earth and the abandonment of the tower. This narrative serves as a reminder of the potential consequences of human hubris and the disruptive power of divine will.

THE TOWER
TOWER OF BABEL

UPRIGHT KEYWORDS:	REVERSED KEYWORDS:
Upheaval	*Fear of change*
Revelation	*Avoiding disaster*
Chaos	*Resisting shock*
Breakdown	*Rebuilding*
Sudden change	

CARD MEANING IN UPRIGHT POSITION:

Sudden and inevitable breakdown or upheaval that, while destructive, offers the opportunity for a new perspective or a fresh start. It symbolizes the dismantling of existing structures due to foundational flaws.

- **Upheaval:** *A sudden, radical change that disrupts the status quo.*
- **Revelation:** *The exposure of deeper truths that were previously hidden.*
- **Chaos:** *A period of disorder and confusion following a shock.*
- **Breakdown:** *The collapse of structures or beliefs that are no longer sustainable.*
- **Sudden Change:** *An unexpected event that forces reevaluation of one's path.*

CARD MEANING IN REVERSED POSITION:

Resistance to change or the postponement of inevitable destruction. It may also signify the process of rebuilding and learning from past upheavals, suggesting a more gradual realization or transformation.

- **Fear of Change:** *Resistance due to fear of the unknown.*
- **Avoiding Disaster:** *Attempts to prevent or delay the inevitable collapse.*
- **Rebuilding:** *The process of recovery and reconstruction after a fall.*
- **Gradual Realization:** *Slowly coming to terms with the need for change.*

"The Tower" card is a powerful allegory for the sudden, transformative events that challenge our foundations and force us to confront our limitations and pride. It underscores the dual nature of destruction: as a harbinger of chaos and a necessary precursor to renewal and growth.

The Star

STAR OF BETHLEHEM

After Jesus was born in Bethlehem in Judea, during the time of King Herod, Magi from the east arrived in Jerusalem, asking, "Where is the One who has been born King of the Jews?
We saw His star in the east and have come to worship Him."
Matthew 2:1-2 BSB

The Star of Bethlehem is a celestial phenomenon mentioned in the Gospel of Matthew, associated with the birth of Jesus Christ. It is described as leading the Magi (wise men) from the East to Jerusalem to celebrate the birth of the "king of the Jews."

The star symbolizes divine intervention in the world and the manifestation of prophecy, guiding those who seek enlightenment and truth.

UPRIGHT KEYWORDS:	REVERSED KEYWORDS:
Hope	*Despair*
Inspiration	*Lack of faith*
Guidance	*Misguidance*
Renewal	*Disillusionment*
Faith	

CARD MEANING IN UPRIGHT POSITION:

Optimism, clarity, and spiritual guidance. It represents the light at the end of the tunnel, offering hope and direction after a difficult time.

- **Hope:** *Feeling optimistic and believing in a positive future.*
- **Inspiration:** *Being motivated to pursue new ideas and opportunities.*
- **Guidance:** *Receiving direction and clarity on one's path.*
- **Renewal:** *Experiencing a sense of rejuvenation and new beginnings.*
- **Faith:** *Trusting in the universe or divine will.*

CARD MEANING IN REVERSED POSITION:

Suggests a loss of hope or faith, feeling misguided or disconnected from one's spiritual path. It can indicate disillusionment or the need to reconnect with one's inner light.

- **Despair:** *Feeling hopeless or overwhelmed by negativity.*
- **Lack of Faith:** *Doubting oneself and one's path.*
- **Misguidance:** *Feeling lost or led astray.*
- **Disillusionment:** *Becoming disenchanted with one's beliefs or life direction.*

"The Star" card is a beacon of divine hope and guidance, leading the way to renewal and faith. This interpretation underscores the importance of looking to the light, even in darkness, and trusting in the journey toward spiritual fulfillment and enlightenment.

The Moon

JACOB'S DREAM AT BETHEL

And Jacob had a dream about a ladder that rested on the earth
with its top reaching up to heaven,
and God's angels were going up and down the ladder.
Genesis 28:12 BSB

THE MOON
JACOB'S DREAM AT BETHEL

Jacob, a key patriarch in the Bible, is known for his complex life full of challenges, transformations, and encounters with the divine. His dream at Bethel is a significant moment of spiritual awakening and promise, where God renews the covenant made with Abraham and Isaac, promising Jacob protection and a multitude of descendants. This story encapsulates the journey from doubt and fear towards faith and understanding, akin to the voyage through the night that The Moon card suggests.

UPRIGHT KEYWORDS:	REVERSED KEYWORDS:
Intuition	*Confusion*
Uncertainty	*Fear*
Subconscious	*Misinterpretation*
Revelation	*Ignoring intuition*
Mystery	

CARD MEANING IN UPRIGHT POSITION:

Symbolizes the need to trust one's intuition and inner guidance when facing uncertainty and the subconscious fears that arise during periods of darkness. It represents the journey towards understanding deeper truths and mysteries.

- **Intuition:** *Trusting in inner guidance to navigate through uncertainty.*
- **Uncertainty:** *Embracing the unknown as a path to growth and enlightenment.*
- **Subconscious:** *Delving into the subconscious for insight and revelation.*
- **Revelation:** *Unveiling hidden truths and gaining deeper spiritual understanding.*
- **Mystery:** *Accepting the mysteries of life and the spiritual journey.*

CARD MEANING IN REVERSED POSITION:

Period of confusion, fear, and anxiety, where one may be misled by illusion or ignore inner wisdom. It suggests a challenge in discerning reality from deception or in overcoming inner doubts.

- **Confusion:** *Feeling lost in the face of ambiguity and uncertainty.*
- **Fear:** *Allowing fear and anxiety to cloud judgment and intuition.*
- **Misinterpretation:** *Misunderstanding signs or messages on the spiritual path.*
- **Ignoring Intuition:** *Neglecting the inner voice.*

"The Moon" card is a narrative of navigating through the depths of the unknown, guided by faith and intuition towards a deeper understanding and connection with the divine. It emphasizes the importance of facing subconscious fears and embracing the mysteries of the spiritual journey to uncover hidden truths and attain enlightenment.

The Sun

TRIUMPHAL ENTRY INTO JERUSALEM

The crowds that went ahead of Him and those that followed were shouting: "Hosanna to the Son of David!" "Blessed is He who comes in the name of the Lord!" "Hosanna in the highest!"
Matthew 21:9 BSB

THE SUN
TRIUMPHAL ENTRY INTO JERUSALEM

The triumphal entry of Jesus into Jerusalem, marks a significant event in Christian tradition, symbolizing Jesus' acknowledgment as king by the people. Riding on a donkey, a humble beast of burden, Jesus entered Jerusalem while crowds spread their cloaks and palm branches on the road, shouting "Hosanna!"—a cry for salvation and a declaration of praise. This moment, fulfilling Old Testament prophecies about the Messiah's arrival, contrasts royal expectations with Jesus' mission of peace and humility. It highlights the dichotomy between worldly power and divine kingship.

UPRIGHT KEYWORDS:	REVERSED KEYWORDS:
Joy	Negativity
Success	Depression
Celebration	Sadness
Positivity	Lack of clarity
Vitality	

CARD MEANING IN UPRIGHT POSITION:

Symbolizes a period of great joy, achievement, and recognition. It signifies clarity of purpose, vitality, and the warmth of success. It represents the fulfillment of a journey and the beginning of a new, enlightened path.

- **Joy:** *Experiencing pure happiness and contentment.*
- **Success:** *Achieving goals and receiving recognition.*
- **Celebration:** *Sharing accomplishments with others in a spirit of happiness.*
- **Positivity:** *Maintaining a positive outlook and radiating warmth to others.*
- **Vitality:** *Feeling full of life and energy, ready to undertake new challenges.*

CARD MEANING IN REVERSED POSITION:

Lack of joy, feeling overshadowed by negativity, or a delay in achieving success and recognition. It suggests a need to rediscover one's inner light and positivity to overcome obstacles.

- **Negativity:** *Feeling overwhelmed by negative thoughts or situations.*
- **Depression:** *Struggling with sadness or lack of motivation.*
- **Sadness:** *Experiencing a temporary lack of joy or success.*
- **Lack of Clarity:** *Facing confusion about one's path or purpose.*

"The Sun" tarot card is a symbol of the light of spirit and truth entering into the heart of human experience, signifying moments of joy, recognition, and the bright clarity of divine love. It invites reflection on the sources of our joy and success, reminding us of the light that guides us through life's journey.

Judgment

LAST JUDGMENT

All the nations will be gathered before Him,
and He will separate the people one from another,
as a shepherd separates the sheep from the goats.
Matthew 25:32 BSB

JUDGMENT
LAST JUDGMENT

The Last Judgment refers to the final and ultimate judgment by God of every individual's deeds in life. It is a moment when the faithful are separated from the unfaithful, leading to either eternal salvation or damnation. This concept emphasizes accountability, the consequences of one's actions, and the possibility of spiritual renewal and redemption.

UPRIGHT KEYWORDS:	REVERSED KEYWORDS:
Rebirth	*Self-doubt*
Inner calling	*Failure to learn lessons*
Absolution	*Delay*
Self-evaluation	*Guilt*
Awakening	

CARD MEANING IN UPRIGHT POSITION:

Time of self-assessment and awakening to one's true purpose. It represents the call to rise to a higher level of consciousness, acknowledging past actions, and moving towards redemption and renewal.

- **Rebirth:** *Experiencing a profound transformation and renewal.*
- **Inner Calling:** *Heeding a powerful call to a higher purpose or existence.*
- **Absolution:** *Releasing guilt and embracing forgiveness for past actions.*
- **Self-Evaluation:** *Reflecting on past behaviors and their impact on one's path.*
- **Awakening:** *Gaining a new understanding of oneself and one's place in the universe.*

CARD MEANING IN REVERSED POSITION:

Period of self-doubt, failure to heed the call to transformation, or lingering guilt over past deeds. It implies a need for introspection to overcome obstacles to personal growth.

- **Self-Doubt:** *Questioning one's ability to change or make amends.*
- **Failure to Learn Lessons:** *Repeating past mistakes due to unacknowledged faults.*
- **Delay:** *Postponing necessary judgment or refusal to face the truth.*
- **Guilt:** *Being held back by unresolved guilt or issues.*

The "Judgment" card portrays the ultimate reckoning and the opportunity for spiritual awakening. It emphasizes the themes of judgment not as condemnation but as a call to higher consciousness, urging reflection on our lives, the acceptance of past actions, and the embrace of a transformative path toward redemption and enlightenment.

The World

NEW JERUSALEM

*I saw the holy city, the new Jerusalem,
coming down out of heaven from God,
prepared as a bride adorned for her husband.*
Revelation 21:2 BSB

THE WORLD
NEW JERUSALEM

The New Jerusalem is a prophetic vision of a heavenly city, signifying the fulfillment of God's promise of a new, perfect world where God dwells with humanity, and there is no more suffering or death. It represents the culmination of the biblical narrative of redemption, the ultimate reunion of the divine with the mortal, and the achievement of eternal peace and glory.

UPRIGHT KEYWORDS:	REVERSED KEYWORDS:
Completion	Incompletion
Fulfillment	Delay
Unity	Lack of closure
Harmony	Stagnation
Accomplishment	

CARD MEANING IN UPRIGHT POSITION:

Achievement of a significant milestone or the completion of a long journey. It stands for wholeness, fulfillment, and the realization of one's goals and desires.

- **Completion:** *Achieving a significant milestone or completing a major phase.*
- **Fulfillment:** *Feeling satisfied and fulfilled at the culmination of efforts.*
- **Unity:** *Experiencing a sense of wholeness and unity with the universe.*
- **Harmony:** *Living in harmony with oneself and the world.*
- **Accomplishment:** *Recognizing and celebrating one's achievements and growth.*

CARD MEANING IN REVERSED POSITION:

Lack of completion, unresolved issues, or delays in achieving a sense of wholeness. It embodies the need to address unfinished business or obstacles that prevent the realization of full potential.

- **Incompletion:** *Experiencing a sense of unfinished business or lack of closure.*
- **Delay:** *Facing delays in the culmination or fulfillment of projects.*
- **Lack of Closure:** *Struggling with unresolved issues that hinder progress.*
- **Stagnation:** *Feeling stuck or unable to move forward.*

"The World" card is a portrayal of divine completion, fulfillment, and the ultimate reunion of heaven and earth. It emphasizes the culmination of spiritual journeys, the achievement of harmony and unity, and the realization of eternal peace and glory as promised in the biblical vision of the future. It invites reflection on our own life's completions and the harmonious integration of our experiences into a whole, fulfilling existence.

CHAPTER 5

Minor Arcana

In the context of the Biblical Tarot, the Minor Arcana cards serve as a detailed exploration of the day-to-day challenges, victories, emotions, and lessons that shape our spiritual journey. While the Major Arcana cards delve into significant life lessons and archetypal themes grounded in biblical stories, the Minor Arcana brings the focus to the more immediate, practical aspects of life, seen through a biblical lens. Each suit within the Minor Arcana - Candles, Chalices, Feathers, and Grains - corresponds to a different element of our experience, reflecting the complexity and variety of human life as mirrored in the narratives and teachings of the Bible.

CANDLES
(Element: Fire)

Candles are associated with creativity, action, and ambition, embodying the soul's drive to manifest and the will to achieve. These narratives encourage us to pursue our goals with faith and courage.

CHALICES
(Element: Water)

The Suit of Chalices is associated with emotions, relationships, and connections. These cards draw from stories of love, family, friendship, and spiritual communion.

FEATHERS
(Element: Air)

The Suit of Feathers deals with intellect, conflict, and moral dilemmas, resonating with the challenges of truth, justice, and ethical decisions. Biblical stories that feature challenges, such as Solomon's wise judgment or the struggles of Paul, illuminate the complexities and mental struggles represented by the Feathers. This suit prompts reflection on how we navigate conflicts and wield the power of truth and intellect.

GRAINS
(Element: Earth)

Grains, connected to the element of Earth, represent material aspects of life such as work, health, and possessions. In a biblical context, these cards could highlight the stewardship of resources, the value of hard work, and the blessings of provision.

The Minor Arcana, through these four suits, offers a nuanced view of the everyday experiences that compose our life's journey, grounded in the wisdom and trials of biblical figures. It speaks to the personal, the immediate, and the practical, encouraging reflection on how we navigate our daily lives within the broader spiritual landscape. Each card, with its unique biblical narrative, acts as a mirror for personal reflection, offering insights into our actions, choices, and emotional and spiritual well-being.

MINOR ARCANA

Candles

Ace of Candles

MOSES AND THE BURNING BUSH

When the LORD saw that he had gone over to look,
God called out to him from within the bush, "Moses, Moses!"
"Here I am," he answered.
Exodus 3:4 BSB

"When the Lord saw that he had gone over to look,
God called to him from within the bush, 'Moses!
Moses!' And Moses said, 'Here I am.' "
Exodus 3:4 (NIV)

ACE *of* CANDLES
MOSES AND THE BURNING BUSH

In the story of Moses and the Burning Bush, Moses encounters God within a miraculously burning bush that is not consumed by the flames. Through this encounter, God calls Moses to lead the Israelites out of Egypt and into freedom, marking the beginning of Moses's spiritual journey and leadership. This moment of divine communication and inspiration is emblematic of the transformative power of faith and purpose.

<u>UPRIGHT KEYWORDS:</u>	<u>REVERSED KEYWORDS:</u>
Inspiration	*Delay*
New beginnings	*Lack of motivation*
Creativity	*Wasted potential*
Enthusiasm	*Uninspired*
Potential	

CARD MEANING IN UPRIGHT POSITION:

Moment of profound inspiration and the beginning of a new adventure or creative project. It represents the potential for growth, the excitement of starting something new, and the courage to take the first step.

- **Inspiration:** *Experiencing a sudden surge of creativity or a new idea.*
- **New Beginnings:** *Starting a new venture or chapter in life with enthusiasm.*
- **Creativity:** *Channeling energy into creative projects or solutions.*
- **Enthusiasm:** *Approaching life with excitement and optimism.*
- **Opportunity:** *Seizing the chance to pursue a passion or calling.*

CARD MEANING IN REVERSED POSITION:

A period of stagnation, missed opportunities, or hesitation to embrace a new beginning. It suggests a need to reignite one's passion and find motivation to overcome obstacles.

- **Delay:** *Experiencing setbacks or slow starts to new projects.*
- **Lack of Motivation:** *Feeling uninspired or apathetic towards new ventures.*
- **Wasted Potential:** *Not utilizing one's talents or missing out on opportunities.*
- **Uninspired:** *Needing a spark to reignite passion and enthusiasm.*

The "Ace of Candles" card is a statement of divine inspiration and the call to embark on a significant life journey. It highlights the moment of ignition—where faith, purpose, and action converge—inviting reflection on our own moments of inspiration and the paths they lead us to pursue.

Two of Candles

ELIJAH ON MOUNT CARMEL

Then Elijah approached all the people and said, "How long will you waver between two opinions? If the LORD is God, follow Him. But if Baal is God, follow him."
1 Kings 18:21 BSB

"Elijah went before the people and said, 'How long will you waver between two opinions? If the Lord is God, follow him; but if Baal is God, follow him.' "
1 Kings 18:21 (NIV)

TWO *of* CANDLES
ELIJAH ON MOUNT CARMEL

Elijah confronts the prophets of Baal on Mount Carmel to prove to the Israelites that the Lord is the true God. Elijah proposes a test involving two altars: one for Baal and one for the Lord. Despite the prophets of Baal's efforts, their god does not answer by fire. Elijah then prepares his altar, drenches it in water, and prays to the Lord, who responds with fire, consuming the sacrifice. This act leads the people to proclaim the Lord as God. The story highlights Elijah's faith, strategic planning, and the bold execution of his vision amidst uncertainty.

UPRIGHT KEYWORDS:	REVERSED KEYWORDS:
Planning	*Fear of unknown*
Future visions	*Indecision*
Decisions	*Over-planning*
Discovery	*Missed opportunities*
Courage	

CARD MEANING IN UPRIGHT POSITION:

Standing at a crossroads with the world in your hands, contemplating a vast horizon of possibilities. It signifies the initial stages of planning or decision-making, with the courage to face the unknown and the wisdom to look forward.

- **Planning:** *Carefully considering the next steps and preparing for the future.*
- **Future Visions:** *Looking ahead with optimism and clarity about one's goals.*
- **Decisions:** *Making strategic choices that will shape the future.*
- **Discovery:** *Being open to new possibilities and adventures.*
- **Courage:** *Having the boldness to take risks and face challenges head-on.*

CARD MEANING IN REVERSED POSITION:

Hesitation, fear of making a wrong decision, or being stuck in the planning phase without taking action. It implies the need to overcome self-doubt and to make a move before opportunities pass by.

- **Fear of Unknown:** *Allowing uncertainty to prevent progress.*
- **Indecision:** *Struggling to make a choice and sticking to it.*
- **Over-Planning:** *Getting caught in the trap of planning without action.*
- **Missed Opportunities:** *Letting chances slip by due to hesitation or fear.*

The "Two of Candles" card is a narrative of faith, strategic foresight, and the courage to act decisively at life's pivotal moments. It underscores the importance of vision and planning in the pursuit of one's goals, as well as the boldness required to venture into the unknown and make significant life decisions.

Three of Candles

THE CALL OF ABRAM

Then the LORD said to Abram,
"Leave your country, your kindred, and your father's household,
and go to the land I will show you.
Genesis 12:1 BSB

"The Lord had said to Abram, 'Go from your country,
your people and your father's household
to the land I will show you.' "
Genesis 12:1 (NIV)

THREE *of* CANDLES
THE CALL OF ABRAM

God calls Abram (later Abraham) to leave his country, his people, and his father's household for a land that God would show him. In return, God promises to make Abram a great nation, to bless him and make his name great. Abram's obedience to God's call, leaving behind everything he knew for the promise of a greater future, marks the beginning of a significant journey not only for Abram but for the formation of a people through whom God would bless all nations.

UPRIGHT KEYWORDS:	REVERSED KEYWORDS:
Expansion	*Obstacles*
Foresight	*Delays*
Progress	*Frustration, resisting change*
Opportunities	*Unfulfilled potential*
Exploration	

CARD MEANING IN UPRIGHT POSITION:

Represents the anticipation and preparation for future ventures and opportunities. It signifies expanding one's horizons, looking forward with optimism, and the readiness to embrace new adventures.

- **Expansion:** *Embracing growth and expanding one's horizons.*
- **Foresight:** *Planning for the future with vision and wisdom.*
- **Progress:** *Moving forward with confidence and anticipation of success.*
- **Opportunities:** *Recognizing and seizing new possibilities.*
- **Exploration:** *Venturing into unknown territories with faith and courage.*

CARD MEANING IN REVERSED POSITION:

Challenges or delays in progress, reluctance to embrace change, or unfulfilled ambitions. It suggests a need to reassess one's path or overcome hesitancy to fully realize potential.

- **Obstacles:** *Encountering delays or barriers to progress.*
- **Delays:** *Experiencing frustration over slowed momentum.*
- **Frustration:** *Feeling hindered in pursuit of goals.*
- **Resisting Change:** *Clinging to the familiar, unwilling to venture forward.*
- **Unfulfilled Potential:** *Hesitating to embrace the full scope of one's abilities or opportunities.*

The "Three of Candles" card is a story of embracing a divinely inspired journey toward a future filled with promise. It shows the importance of faith, vision, and the willingness to step into the unknown, trusting in the fulfillment of promises and the expansion of one's life towards uncharted territories.

Four of Candles

THE ARK BROUGHT TO JERUSALEM

And David, wearing a linen ephod, danced with all his might before the LORD, 15while he and all the house of Israel brought up the ark of the LORD with shouting and the sounding of the ram's horn.
2 Samuel 6:14-16 BSB

"Wearing a linen ephod, David was dancing before the Lord with all his might, while he and all Israel were bringing up the ark of the Lord with shouts and the sound of trumpets."
2 Samuel 6:14-16 (NIV)
FOUR of CANDLES
THE ARK BROUGHT TO JERUSALEM

David successfully brings the Ark of the Covenant to Jerusalem, marking a significant religious and cultural milestone for the Israelites. The Ark's arrival in Jerusalem is met with great celebration, including music, dancing, and offerings. This event not only symbolizes God's presence among the people but also unites them in a collective expression of faith and joy. The story reflects the establishment of Jerusalem as the spiritual center and a collective homecoming for the people of Israel.

UPRIGHT KEYWORDS:	REVERSED KEYWORDS:
Celebration	*Lack of support*
Harmony	*Feeling unwelcome*
Community	*Instability*
Homecoming	*Neglected gratitude*
Prosperity	

CARD MEANING IN UPRIGHT POSITION:

Indicates a time of joyous celebration and the fruition of hard work, often involving community or family gatherings. It signifies stability, the establishment of a happy home or community, and the satisfaction of achieving communal goals.

- **Celebration:** *Marking a significant achievement or milestone with joy.*
- **Harmony:** *Experiencing peace and unity within a community or family.*
- **Community:** *Coming together to share successes and support one another.*
- **Homecoming:** *Returning to or finding a spiritual or emotional home.*
- **Prosperity:** *Enjoying the rewards of collective efforts and faith.*

CARD MEANING IN REVERSED POSITION:

Feelings of isolation, lack of support, or the breakdown of harmony within a group. It suggests a need to rebuild foundational relationships or address issues that prevent a sense of belonging and stability.

- **Lack of Support:** *Feeling isolated or without community backing.*
- **Feeling Unwelcome:** *Struggling to find one's place within a group or family.*
- **Instability:** *Experiencing disruption in harmony or a sense of belonging.*
- **Neglected Gratitude:** *Overlooking the blessings and support of others.*

The "Four of Candles" card is a celebration of community, unity, and the blessings of shared faith and prosperity. It highlights the importance of coming together to celebrate achievements and establish a sense of belonging and harmony within a communal or familial space.

Five of Candles

JOSEPH AND HIS JEALOUS BROTHERS

Come, let us sell him to the Ishmaelites and not lay a hand on him;
for he is our brother, our own flesh."
And they agreed.
Genesis 37:27 BSB

" *'Come, let's sell him to the Ishmaelites and not lay*
our hands on him; after all, he is our brother, our own
flesh and blood.' His brothers agreed."
Genesis 37:27 (NIV)

FIVE *of* CANDLES
JOSEPH AND HIS JEALOUS BROTHERS

Joseph, the favored son of Jacob, is envied by his brothers because of the special treatment he receives from their father and because of Joseph's dreams that predict his rise to prominence over them. Their jealousy leads them to sell Joseph into slavery. However, this act of betrayal begins Joseph's journey from slave to high-ranking official in Egypt, where he eventually reconciles with his family during a famine. The story encapsulates the complexity of familial relationships, personal growth through adversity, and the ultimate reconciliation and understanding.

UPRIGHT KEYWORDS:	REVERSED KEYWORDS:
Conflict	*Resolution*
Competition	*Avoidance of conflict*
Tension	*Learning from challenges*
Struggles	*Seeking common ground*
Diversity of thought	

CARD MEANING IN UPRIGHT POSITION:

Competition, conflicts, or clashes of personalities. It signifies a period of struggle that, while challenging, is typically not insurmountable and can lead to growth through overcoming adversity.

- **Conflict:** *Experiencing disagreements or competition, possibly from misunderstandings or differing goals.*
- **Competition:** *Engaging in healthy rivalry that pushes for improvement.*
- **Tension:** *Navigating a period of stress due to clashing interests.*
- **Struggles:** *Overcoming obstacles that arise from external pressures.*
- **Diversity of Thought:** *Recognizing the value in differing perspectives, even if it leads to temporary conflict.*

CARD MEANING IN REVERSED POSITION:

Moving past conflicts, learning valuable lessons from challenges, or the necessity to find harmony and common ground amidst diversity. It hints at a period of cooling tensions and seeking solutions.

- **Resolution:** *Finding solutions to conflicts and moving forward.*
- **Avoidance of Conflict:** *Choosing to step back from unnecessary battles.*
- **Learning from Challenges:** *Gaining insights and growth from past struggles.*
- **Seeking Common Ground:** *Emphasizing collaboration and harmony over competition.*

The "Five of Candles" card represents familial conflict, personal growth through adversity, and the transformative power of forgiveness and reconciliation. It underscores the potential for constructive competition and the importance of overcoming challenges to achieve unity and understanding.

Six of Candles

THE FALL OF JERICHO

*When they heard the blast of the horn, the people gave a great shout,
and the wall collapsed.
Then all the people charged straight into the city and captured it.*
Joshua 6:20 BSB

In Joshua 6, the Israelites, led by Joshua, conquer the city of Jericho in a miraculous manner. God commands the Israelites to march around the city walls once a day for six days with the priests carrying the Ark of the Covenant and blowing trumpets. On the seventh day, after marching around the city seven times and with a long blast on the trumpets, the Israelites shout, and the walls of Jericho collapse, allowing them to take the city. This story symbolizes the power of divine intervention and the triumph of faith over seemingly insurmountable obstacles.

"When the trumpets sounded, the army shouted, and at the sound of the trumpet, when the men gave a loud shout, the wall collapsed; so everyone charged straight in, and they took the city."
Joshua 6:20 (NIV)

SIX *of* CANDLES
THE FALL OF JERICHO

UPRIGHT KEYWORDS:	REVERSED KEYWORDS:
Victory	*Delayed success*
Success	*Lack of recognition*
Leadership	*Arrogance*
Acclaim	*Fall from grace*
Achievement	

CARD MEANING IN UPRIGHT POSITION:

Triumph and recognition after overcoming challenges. It represents the celebration of achievements and the acknowledgment of one's leadership and success by others.

- **Victory:** *Achieving success after facing and overcoming obstacles.*
- **Success:** *Fulfilling one's goals and receiving acclaim for one's efforts.*
- **Leadership:** *Demonstrating leadership that guides to collective success.*
- **Acclaim:** *Being publicly recognized and celebrated for one's achievements.*
- **Achievement:** *The culmination of hard work and strategy leading to a desired outcome.*
-

CARD MEANING IN REVERSED POSITION:

Struggle with receiving due recognition, experiencing delays in achieving results, or dealing with the consequences of arrogance. It suggests a need for introspection on one's journey to success.

- **Delayed Success:** *Experiencing setbacks on the path to achievement.*
- **Lack of Recognition:** *Achievements going unnoticed or unappreciated by others.*
- **Arrogance:** *Allowing success to lead to overconfidence or disregard for others.*
- **Fall from Grace:** *The potential downfall that can follow unchecked pride or neglect of foundational values.*

The "Six of Candles" card is a narrative of achieving victory through faith, leadership, and the collective effort of a community guided by divine will. It emphasizes the joy of success and the importance of humility and gratitude in the face of triumph, reminding us of the strength found in faith and obedience.

Seven of Candles

DAVID AND GOLIATH

But David said to the Philistine,
"You come against me with sword and spear and javelin,
but I come against you in the name of the LORD of Hosts,
the God of the armies of Israel, whom you have defied.
1 Samuel 17:45 BSB

In the story of David and Goliath (1 Samuel 17), the young shepherd David faces the Philistine giant Goliath, who has been terrorizing the Israelite army. Despite Goliath's formidable size and strength, and the fact that David is armed only with a sling and a few stones, David's faith in God gives him the courage to confront and defeat Goliath. David's victory serves as a profound demonstration of faith, courage, and the power of God working through an individual to overcome seemingly insurmountable odds.

"David said to the Philistine, 'You come against me with sword and spear and javelin, but I come against you in the name of the Lord Almighty, the God of the armies of Israel, whom you have defied.' "
1 Samuel 17:45 (NIV)

SEVEN *of* CANDLES
DAVID AND GOLIATH

UPRIGHT KEYWORDS:	REVERSED KEYWORDS:
Courage	*Overwhelm*
Perseverance	*Giving up*
Challenge	*Defensiveness*
Defense	*Vulnerability*
Determination	

CARD MEANING IN UPRIGHT POSITION:

Facing challenges head-on with courage and determination. It signifies standing up for what you believe in, even when faced with opposition or adversity, and the perseverance needed to overcome obstacles.

- **Courage:** *Demonstrating bravery in the face of daunting challenges.*
- **Perseverance:** *Continuing to fight or stand up for oneself despite obstacles.*
- **Challenge:** *Confronting and overcoming opposition or adversity.*
- **Defense:** *Protecting one's beliefs or standing against external pressures.*
- **Determination:** *Showing resolve and strength of character to succeed.*

CARD MEANING IN REVERSED POSITION:

Feeling overwhelmed by challenges or opposition, possibly leading to a retreat or surrender. It implies a need to reassess one's strategies or to find inner strength to face difficulties.

- **Overwhelm:** *Feeling daunted by the scale of challenges faced.*
- **Giving Up:** *Considering retreat in the face of opposition.*
- **Defensiveness:** *Reacting to perceived threats with unnecessary force.*
- **Vulnerability:** *Experiencing a sense of exposure or weakness.*

The "Seven of Candles" tarot card is all about overcoming great challenges through faith, courage, and strategic thinking. It emphasizes the importance of inner strength, the courage to stand up against formidable challenges, and the power of faith to guide and protect in times of adversity.

Eight of Candles

PHILIP AND THE ETHIOPIAN

When they came up out of the water, the Spirit of the Lord carried Philip away, and the eunuch saw him no more, but went on his way rejoicing.
Acts 8:39 BSB

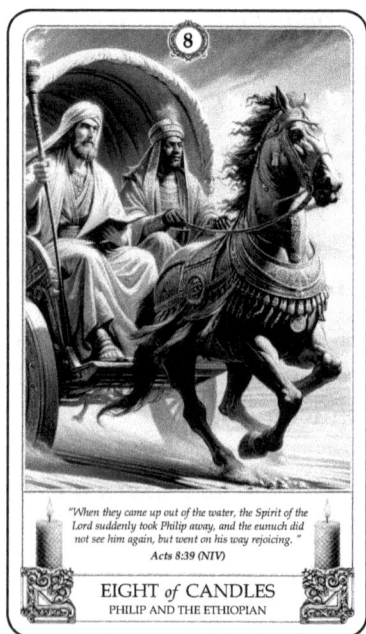

In Acts 8:26-40, Philip, is directed by an angel of the Lord to go south to the road that descends from Jerusalem to Gaza. There, he encounters an Ethiopian eunuch, a high official under the queen of the Ethiopians, reading the Book of Isaiah. Guided by the Spirit, Philip joins the eunuch in his chariot, explains the scriptures to him, and baptizes him. The story illustrates the rapid spread of the Christian message and the immediate response of those who hear and understand it.

"When they came up out of the water, the Spirit of the Lord suddenly took Philip away, and the eunuch did not see him again, but went on his way rejoicing."
Acts 8:39 (NIV)

EIGHT of CANDLES
PHILIP AND THE ETHIOPIAN

UPRIGHT KEYWORDS:	REVERSED KEYWORDS:
Speed	Delays
Movement	Frustration
Swift action	Stagnation
Quick changes	Miscommunication
Communication	Impatience

CARD MEANING IN UPRIGHT POSITION:

Rapid progress or the swift unfolding of events. It signifies clear communication, the quick advancement of projects, and the immediate action inspired by divine or intuitive guidance.

- **Speed:** *Events or projects progressing rapidly.*
- **Movement:** *Advancement and forward momentum in various aspects of life.*
- **Swift Action:** *Taking immediate and decisive action.*
- **Quick Changes:** *Experiencing sudden shifts or transformations.*
- **Communication:** *Receiving or delivering messages clearly and quickly.*

CARD MEANING IN REVERSED POSITION:

Obstacles to progress, or confusion in communication. It depicts a time of waiting or frustration, where actions are impeded, and messages may be misunderstood.

- **Delays:** *Experiencing setbacks that slow progress.*
- **Frustration:** *Feeling hindered by obstacles or lack of movement.*
- **Stagnation:** *A period of inactivity or slow development.*
- **Miscommunication:** *Misunderstandings or unclear information exchange.*
- **Impatience:** *Feeling restless or eager for progress that isn't happening.*

The "Eight of Candles" card illustrates the divine orchestration, leading to rapid spiritual growth and the swift spread of enlightenment. It demonstrates the power of being open to divine guidance, the importance of timely action, and the impact of clear, inspired communication on the journey of faith.

Nine of Candles

SATAN TESTS JOB

In all this, Job did not sin
or charge God with wrongdoing.
Job 1:22 BSB

"In all this, Job did not sin
by charging God with wrongdoing."
Job 1:22 (NIV)

NINE *of* CANDLES
SATAN TESTS JOB

The story of Job (found in the Book of Job) revolves around a righteous man named Job, whose faith is tested by Satan with God's permission. Job suffers tremendous loss, including his wealth, health, and family, yet he refuses to give up on God. Despite the advice of his friends and the urging of his wife, Job maintains his faith, questioning God's reasons but never renouncing his faithfulness. Ultimately, God restores Job's fortunes, doubling what he had before, as a reward for his steadfast faith.

UPRIGHT KEYWORDS:	REVERSED KEYWORDS:
Resilience	Weariness
Perseverance	Exhaustion
Endurance	Defensiveness
Guardedness	Paranoia
Readiness	Breakdown

CARD MEANING IN UPRIGHT POSITION:

Resilience and determination in the face of challenges. It signifies being on the verge of completion or success after enduring hardships, maintaining faith and strength despite weariness.

- **Resilience:** *Demonstrating strength and endurance through difficult times.*
- **Perseverance:** *Continuing to push forward despite setbacks.*
- **Endurance:** *Holding onto one's beliefs or goals with unwavering faith.*
- **Guardedness:** *Being cautious for further challenges and obstacles.*
- **Readiness:** *Staying prepared for what comes next.*

CARD MEANING IN REVERSED POSITION:

Indicates nearing a point of exhaustion, where the continued struggle may lead to a loss of faith or strength. It proposes reassessing one's defenses and perhaps finding new strategies or seeking support.

- **Weariness:** *Feeling overwhelmed by continuous struggles.*
- **Exhaustion:** *Nearing the limit of one's strength or faith.*
- **Defensiveness:** *Becoming overly protective or closed off.*
- **Paranoia:** *Letting fear of further challenges hinder progress.*
- **Breakdown:** *The potential collapse of resolve or spirit due to unrelenting pressure.*

The "Nine of Candles" card is a story of unwavering faith and resilience in the face of profound trials. It focuses on the courage to stand firm in one's convictions, the endurance needed to navigate life's darkest moments, and the ultimate vindication that comes from steadfast perseverance and trust in one's spiritual beliefs.

Ten of Candles

JEREMIAH'S BURDEN

Why did I come out of the womb to see only trouble and sorrow,
and to end my days in shame?
Jeremiah 20:18 BSB

"Why did I ever come out of the womb to see trouble
and sorrow and to end my days in shame?"
Jeremiah 20:18 (NIV)

TEN *of* CANDLES
JEREMIAH'S BURDEN

Jeremiah, often called the "weeping prophet," was tasked by God to prophesy the destruction of Judah and Jerusalem due to their unfaithfulness. His messages were met with hostility, rejection, and persecution, making his prophetic mission a heavy burden. Despite the emotional and physical toll, Jeremiah remained committed to his divine calling, enduring great personal suffering to fulfill God's command. His life reflects the struggles of bearing a heavy load for the sake of a higher purpose.

UPRIGHT KEYWORDS:	REVERSED KEYWORDS:
Burden	*Release*
Responsibility	*Delegation*
Struggle	*Unburdening*
Perseverance	*Overcoming adversity*
Duty	*Learning to let go*

CARD MEANING IN UPRIGHT POSITION:

Bearing heavy burdens, whether they are responsibilities, obligations, or the weight of one's duties. It represents the perseverance needed to carry through with one's tasks, despite feeling overwhelmed.

- **Burden:** *Carrying a heavy load, whether emotional, physical, or spiritual.*
- **Responsibility:** *Facing duties and obligations with determination.*
- **Struggle:** *Enduring hardships and challenges in fulfilling one's commitments.*
- **Perseverance:** *Continuing to move forward despite feeling weighed down.*
- **Duty:** *Commitment to a task, regardless of the cost.*

CARD MEANING IN REVERSED POSITION:

Indicates a potential release from burdens, whether through delegating tasks, finding relief from stress, or learning from past struggles to avoid being overwhelmed in the future. It suggests a period of lightening one's load and finding a way to manage responsibilities more effectively.

- **Release:** *Finding relief from heavy burdens and stress.*
- **Delegation:** *Learning to share responsibilities*
- **Unburdening:** *Letting go of unnecessary weights.*
- **Overcoming Adversity:** *Learning from challenges to navigate future obstacles more effectively.*
- **Learning to Let Go:** *Recognizing when to release oneself from overwhelming duties.*

The "Ten of Candles" card represents the profound weight of responsibility, alongside the struggle and resilience required to uphold one's duty in the face of adversity. It calls attention to the importance of perseverance and faithfulness, while also acknowledging the relief and growth that come from overcoming or learning to manage one's burdens.

Page of Candles

MIRIAM'S PRAISE FOR GOD

And Miriam sang back to them:
"Sing to the LORD, for He is highly exalted;
the horse and rider He has thrown into the sea."
Exodus 15:21 BSB

After the Israelites successfully crossed the Red Sea and escaped the pursuing Egyptian army, Miriam, the prophetess and sister of Moses and Aaron, led the people in a song and dance of praise to God for their deliverance. This act of worship and celebration, underscores the power of faith and the joy of salvation. Miriam's response to God's miraculous intervention showcases her leadership in worship and her role as a conduit of inspiration and praise among her people.

UPRIGHT KEYWORDS:	REVERSED KEYWORDS:
Inspiration	*Hesitation*
Enthusiasm	*Lack of direction*
Discovery	*Stifled creativity*
Creativity	*Pessimism*
New beginnings	

CARD MEANING IN UPRIGHT POSITION:

Beginning of a new adventure filled with excitement and the willingness to express oneself boldly and creatively. It portrays a call to adventure, the spark of inspiration, and the eagerness to take on new challenges.

- **Inspiration:** *Feeling motivated and energized by new ideas or opportunities.*
- **Enthusiasm:** *Approaching life with excitement and openness to new experiences.*
- **Discovery:** *Exploring new paths and learning from the journey.*
- **Creativity:** *Expressing oneself freely.*
- **New Beginnings:** *Embarking on a new phase with optimism and faith.*

CARD MEANING IN REVERSED POSITION:

A phase where enthusiasm is dampened by hesitation or doubt, where creative expression is hindered, or where there is a lack of clarity about one's path. It conveys the need to rediscover one's passion and purpose.

- **Hesitation:** *Delaying action due to uncertainty or fear.*
- **Lack of Direction:** *Feeling unsure about which path to take.*
- **Stifled Creativity:** *Struggling to express oneself or to find an outlet for one's talents.*
- **Pessimism:** *Letting doubt overshadow enthusiasm and potential.*

The "Page of Candles" card is a depiction of embracing new beginnings with joy and faith. It emphasizes the importance of expressing gratitude and celebration for life's victories, big or small, and the role of inspiration and creativity in guiding us through new chapters in our lives.

Knight of Candles

JOSHUA - LEADER OF FAITH

Have I not commanded you to be strong and courageous?
Do not be afraid; do not be discouraged,
for the LORD your God is with you wherever you go."
Joshua 1:9 BSB

Joshua, the successor to Moses, was charged with leading the Israelites into Canaan, the Promised Land. Under his leadership, the Israelites experienced miraculous victories, including the fall of Jericho, showcasing Joshua's unwavering faith in God's promises. His story, notably his courage to act upon God's commands and his role in fulfilling the divine plan, highlights the qualities of leadership, faith, and the willingness to embark on a challenging journey despite the obstacles.

UPRIGHT KEYWORDS:	REVERSED KEYWORDS:
Action	*Recklessness*
Adventure	*Haste*
Courage	*Aggression*
Passion	*Frustration*
Determination	*Delay*

CARD MEANING IN UPRIGHT POSITION:

Taking bold actions and moving forward with confidence in pursuit of one's goals. It expresses the energy and enthusiasm to tackle challenges head-on, fueled by passion and conviction.

- **Action:** *Taking decisive steps towards achieving one's goals.*
- **Adventure:** *Embarking on a journey filled with challenges and opportunities for growth.*
- **Courage:** *Facing obstacles with bravery and a strong sense of purpose.*
- **Passion:** *Pursuing one's ambitions with enthusiasm.*
- **Determination:** *Demonstrating a steadfast commitment to one's mission.*

CARD MEANING IN REVERSED POSITION:

Impulsiveness or taking unnecessary risks without proper foresight. It points to the frustration from blocked actions or the consequences of hasty decisions, calling for a reassessment of one's approach.

- **Recklessness:** *Acting without considering the consequences, leading to potential pitfalls.*
- **Haste:** *Rushing into situations without proper planning or reflection.*
- **Aggression:** *Allowing one's drive to achieve goals to become confrontational or harmful.*
- **Frustration:** *Experiencing setbacks or delays that impede progress.*
- **Delay:** *Facing obstacles that require patience and a reconsideration of tactics.*

The "Knight of Candles" card is an instance of fearless leadership and the bold pursuit of one's divine calling. It emphasizes the importance of courage and action in the face of adversity, focusing on the dynamic energy required to manifest one's vision while also cautioning against the potential pitfalls of recklessness and haste.

Queen of Candles

DEBORAH - PROPHETESS AND LEADER

*Now Deborah, a prophetess, the wife of Lappidoth,
was judging Israel at that time.*
Judges 4:4 BSB

"*Now Deborah, a prophetess, the wife of Lappidoth,
was leading Israel at that time.*"
Judges 4:4 (NIV)

QUEEN *of* CANDLES
DEBORAH - PROPHETESS AND LEADER

Deborah, one of the major judges of Israel, was a prophetess and the only female judge mentioned in the Bible. She led Israel at a time of oppression and commanded Barak to lead an army against the Canaanite king Jabin and his military commander Sisera. Deborah's leadership and faith in God's command led to a significant victory for Israel. Her story is celebrated in the "Song of Deborah," a victory hymn that praises God for the triumph over the Canaanites, showcasing her wisdom, courage, and effective leadership.

UPRIGHT KEYWORDS:	REVERSED KEYWORDS:
Confidence	*Domineering*
Independence	*Intolerance*
Leadership	*Impatience*
Charisma	*Overbearing*
Determination	*Vindictiveness*

CARD MEANING IN UPRIGHT POSITION:

Depicts a strong character, leadership, confidence and charisma. This individual is independent, energetic, and driven by a deep sense of purpose, inspiring others through their passion and determination.

- **Confidence:** *Self-assurance and belief in one's abilities.*
- **Independence:** *Demonstrating self-reliance and the ability to take charge.*
- **Leadership:** *Guiding others with wisdom, charisma, and vision.*
- **Charisma:** *Attracting and inspiring others through one's energy and enthusiasm.*
- **Determination:** *Pursuing goals with unwavering resolve and courage.*

CARD MEANING IN REVERSED POSITION:

Indicates a tendency towards being domineering or intolerant, possibly using one's strength of character and leadership in a counterproductive way. It conveys a need to temper assertiveness with empathy and patience.

- **Domineering:** *Exercising control in an overbearing manner.*
- **Intolerance and impatience:** *Showing a lack of understanding or patience with others.*
- **Overbearing:** *Overwhelming others with one's presence or opinions.*
- **Vindictiveness:** *Holding grudges or being overly punitive in leadership.*

The "Queen of Candles" card is an example of formidable leadership, charismatic authority, and the fiery spirit of independence. It emphasizes the power of leading with conviction and the impact of a strong, confident individual who inspires others while also cautioning against the shadow aspects of strength, such as the potential for intolerance or impatience.

King of Candles

KING DAVID

I have been with you wherever you have gone,
and I have cut off all your enemies from before you.
Now I will make for you a name like that of the greatest in the land.
2 Samuel 7:9 BSB

"I have been with you wherever you have gone, and I have cut off all your enemies from before you. Now I will make your name great, like the names of the greatest men on earth."
2 Samuel 7:9 (NIV)

KING of CANDLES
KING DAVID

David's rise from shepherd boy to the King of Israel is a story of divine favor, personal bravery, and strategic brilliance. David gains fame by defeating Goliath, earns the love of the people, and navigates the complex political landscape of his time with astuteness. His reign is marked by military conquests and cultural achievements - his poetic psalms. However, David's life is also fraught with personal failings, including his affair with Bathsheba and the resultant turmoil within his own family, illustrating the dual nature of his legacy as both a revered leader and a flawed man.

UPRIGHT KEYWORDS:	REVERSED KEYWORDS:
Leadership	Tyranny
Vision	Impulsiveness
Courage	Overbearing
Charisma	Unfulfilled promises
Creativity	Lack of restraint

CARD MEANING IN UPRIGHT POSITION:

Represents a figure of authority who leads with vision and creativity. This individual is dynamic, bold, and influential, inspiring others through their passion, integrity, and innovative approach to challenges.

- **Leadership:** *Exercising power with wisdom and integrity.*
- **Charisma:** *Drawing others in with compelling charm and confidence.*
- **Courage:** *Facing challenges with bravery and a clear sense of purpose.*
- **Vision:** *Holding a broad perspective and long-term goals.*
- **Creativity:** *Using innovative solutions and creative talents to lead.*

CARD MEANING IN REVERSED POSITION:

A person who may be prone to excesses, misuse of power, or failure to live up to their ideals. It suggests the potential for arrogance, impulsiveness, or a tendency to dominate rather than inspire.

- **Tyranny:** *Misusing power or controlling others oppressively.*
- **Impulsiveness:** *Making hasty decisions without thorough consideration.*
- **Overbearing:** *Dominating discussions or decisions, stifling others' contributions.*
- **Unfulfilled Promises:** *Failing to deliver on commitments or to realize potential.*

The "King of Candles" card is a statement of dynamic leadership, rich in creative energy and the complexities of wielding power. It focuses on the balance required to lead with courage and vision, acknowledging both the inspiring and the cautionary aspects of leadership as demonstrated in David's life.

MINOR ARCANA

Chalices

Ace of Chalices

SAMARITAN WOMAN AT THE WELL

..But whoever drinks the water I give him will never thirst.
Indeed, the water I give him will become in him
a fount of water springing up to eternal life."
John 4:14 BSB

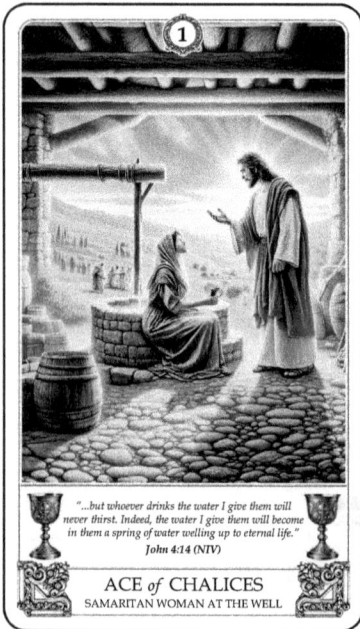

"...but whoever drinks the water I give them will
never thirst. Indeed, the water I give them will become
in them a spring of water welling up to eternal life."
John 4:14 (NIV)

ACE *of* CHALICES
SAMARITAN WOMAN AT THE WELL

Jesus, traveling through Samaria, stops at Jacob's well, where He encounters a Samaritan woman. In the course of their conversation, Jesus reveals knowledge, which astonishes her, and speaks of offering "living water" that would forever quench her thirst. This encounter transforms the woman, who goes on to share her experience with others in her community, leading many to believe in Jesus. The story is a powerful depiction of Jesus's compassion, the breaking of social barriers, and the offer of spiritual awakening and redemption.

UPRIGHT KEYWORDS:	REVERSED KEYWORDS:
Emotional renewal	*Emotional loss*
Spiritual fulfillment	*Blocked creativity*
Love	*Emptiness*
Compassion	*Unfulfilled desires*
Intuition	

CARD MEANING IN UPRIGHT POSITION:

Emotional and spiritual awakening. It sums up the joy of new beginnings, the flow of emotions, and the deep connection to one's intuition and inner truth.

- **Emotional Renewal:** *Experiencing a resurgence of feelings and empathy.*
- **Spiritual Fulfillment:** *Finding a deep sense of peace and purpose.*
- **Love:** *Opening one's heart to receive and give love unconditionally.*
- **Compassion:** *Extending understanding and kindness to oneself and others.*
- **Intuition:** *Trusting one's inner guidance and feelings.*

CARD MEANING IN REVERSED POSITION:

Indicates a time when one may feel emotionally drained or out of touch with their spiritual path. It expresses a need to reconnect with one's inner source of love and fulfillment.

- **Emotional Loss:** *Feeling a sense of emptiness or disconnection from others.*
- **Blocked Creativity:** *Experiencing a lack of inspiration or a creative block.*
- **Emptiness:** *Facing a void where emotional and spiritual fulfillment should be.*
- **Unfulfilled Desires:** *Longing for a connection or purpose that seems out of reach.*

The "Ace of Chalices" card features themes of divine love, emotional transformation, and the offer of a new beginning that promises fulfillment and spiritual enlightenment. It emphasizes the boundless compassion and understanding available to all who open their hearts to new emotional experiences and spiritual truths.

Two of Chalices

THE BOND OF DAVID AND JONATHAN

Then Jonathan made a covenant with David
because he loved him as himself.
1 Samuel 18:3 BSB

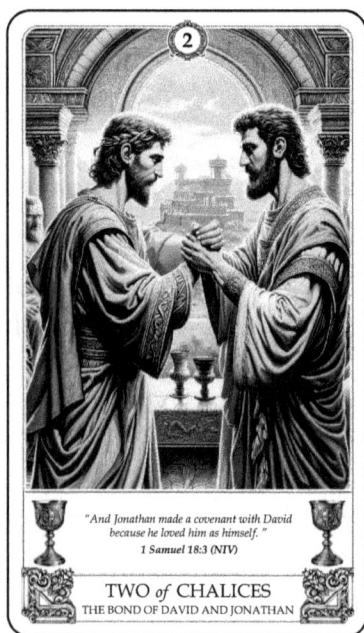

"And Jonathan made a covenant with David because he loved him as himself."
1 Samuel 18:3 (NIV)

TWO *of* CHALICES
THE BOND OF DAVID AND JONATHAN

The friendship between David and Jonathan is one of the most significant relationships in the Bible, depicted in the Books of 1 Samuel. Jonathan, the son of King Saul, and David, who would become Israel's greatest king, formed an immediate and strong bond. Despite Saul's jealousy of David and his attempts to kill him, Jonathan's loyalty to David never wavered. Their story is a testament to loyalty, sacrifice, and an unbreakable emotional bond that transcends familial ties and political intrigue.

UPRIGHT KEYWORDS:	REVERSED KEYWORDS:
Union	*Imbalance*
Partnership	*Broken communication*
Mutual affection	*Tension*
Harmony	*Estrangement*
Cooperation	

CARD MEANING IN UPRIGHT POSITION:

Represents a strong, balanced, and harmonious relationship built on mutual respect, affection, and understanding. It embodies the coming together of individuals who support and elevate each other.

- **Union:** *The joining of two individuals in a relationship that is mutually beneficial and supportive.*
- **Partnership:** *A collaboration based on shared goals, interests, and emotional connection.*
- **Mutual Affection:** *A deep and abiding love and respect for each other.*
- **Harmony:** *A relationship characterized by peace, understanding, and cooperation.*
- **Cooperation:** *Working together seamlessly towards common objectives.*

CARD MEANING IN REVERSED POSITION:

Issues within a relationship that may stem from misunderstandings, lack of communication, or external pressures leading to disharmony or estrangement. It suggests a need to address these issues to restore balance and understanding.

- **Imbalance:** *One party feeling more invested or valued than the other.*
- **Broken Communication:** *Misunderstandings or lack of open dialogue leading to tension.*
- **Tension:** *Underlying issues that disrupt the harmony of the relationship.*
- **Estrangement:** *A distancing within the relationship, either emotionally or physically.*

The "Two of Chalices" card sums up the deep emotional connection, loyalty, and the strength found in true partnership. It emphasizes the power of unity and mutual support, reminding us of the importance of fostering relationships that are rooted in mutual respect, understanding, and unconditional support.

Three of Chalices

THE WEDDING AT CANA

...and the master of the banquet tasted the water that had been turned into wine. He did not know where it was from, but the servants who had drawn the water knew.
John 2:9 BSB

"... and the master of the banquet tasted the water that had been turned into wine."
John 2:9 (NIV)

THREE *of* CHALICES
THE WEDDING AT CANA

At the Wedding at Cana, Jesus, His mother Mary, and His disciples are guests. When the wine runs out, Mary tells Jesus, prompting Him to perform a miracle. Jesus instructs the servants to fill jars with water, which He then turns into wine, not only solving the problem but providing wine of superior quality. This act not only saves the hosts from social embarrassment but also reveals Jesus's divine power to His disciples, deepening their faith. The story is celebrated as a sign of Jesus's glory and His ability to transform the mundane into the extraordinary.

UPRIGHT KEYWORDS:	REVERSED KEYWORDS:
Celebration	*Overindulgence*
Community	*Gossip*
Joy	*Isolation*
Friendship	*Lack of harmony*
Abundance	*Excess*

CARD MEANING IN UPRIGHT POSITION:

Joyous celebration, coming together in friendship and community, and the sharing of achievements and happiness. It symbolizes moments of emotional fulfillment and the beauty of harmonious relationships.

- **Celebration:** *Enjoying moments of joy and celebration with friends and loved ones.*
- **Community:** *Feeling connected to a community or group, sharing in mutual support and happiness.*
- **Friendship:** *Cherishing and nurturing friendships, enjoying the company of others.*
- **Abundance:** *Recognizing and appreciating the abundance in one's life, whether in relationships, love, or material blessings.*

CARD MEANING IN REVERSED POSITION:

Potential issues such as feeling left out, indulging in excess, or experiencing discord within one's social circle. It conveys a need to reevaluate one's social interactions or to find balance in celebration and daily life.

- **Overindulgence:** *Experiencing the consequences of excess, whether in partying, emotions, or material pursuits.*
- **Gossip:** *Getting caught up in social drama or negative talk that harms relationships.*
- **Isolation:** *Feeling disconnected or alienated from one's community or friends.*
- **Lack of Harmony:** *Encountering discord in relationships or within social groups.*

The "Three of Chalices" card is a story of divine celebration and the transformative power of joy and fellowship. It highlights the significance of coming together in happiness and the miraculous possibilities that such unity can bring, as well as the importance of moderation and harmony within communal joy.

Four of Chalices

JONAH'S ANGER

And now, O LORD, please take my life from me,
for it is better for me to die than to live."
Jonah 4:3 BSB

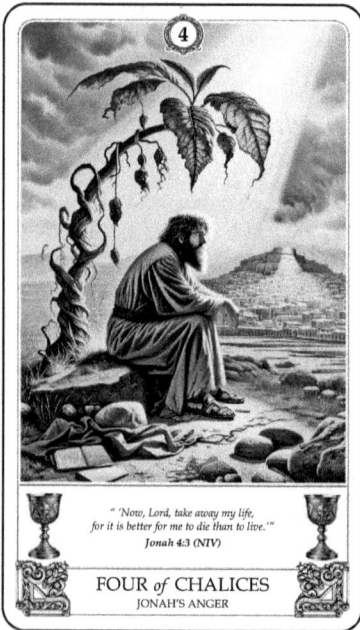

After Jonah finally obeys God's command to warn Nineveh of impending destruction, the city repents, and God spares it. Rather than rejoicing in the mercy shown, Jonah becomes angry and frustrated with God's compassion towards the Ninevites. He retreats outside the city, hoping to witness its destruction, and laments his own discomfort under a withering plant that had provided him shade. God then questions Jonah's anger, and points out Jonah's lack of compassion for the people of Nineveh. The story illustrates Jonah's struggle with accepting God's will and the lesson of divine mercy and compassion.

UPRIGHT KEYWORDS:	REVERSED KEYWORDS:
Discontent	*New perspective*
Apathy	*Gratitude*
Reevaluation	*Acceptance*
Missed opportunities	*Embracing change*
Introspection	

CARD MEANING IN UPRIGHT POSITION:

Self-reflection marked by dissatisfaction or a lack of fulfillment. It constitutes the need to reevaluate one's circumstances and the potential for growth through recognizing overlooked opportunities.

- **Discontent:** *Feeling unsatisfied with one's current situation or emotional state.*
- **Apathy:** *Experiencing a lack of interest in or enthusiasm for what is offered.*
- **Reevaluation:** *Contemplating one's desires and motivations to find true fulfillment.*
- **Missed Opportunities:** *Overlooking potential blessings or chances for improvement.*
- **Introspection:** *Engaging in self-reflection to understand underlying feelings of dissatisfaction.*

CARD MEANING IN REVERSED POSITION:

A shift towards gratitude and the acceptance of new possibilities. It implies moving past apathy or discontent to embrace a fuller appreciation of life's blessings and changes.

- **New Perspective:** *Seeing things in a new light and recognizing previously missed opportunities.*
- **Gratitude:** *Cultivating thankfulness for what one has and for new chances.*
- **Acceptance:** *Embracing the present and opening up to change and growth.*
- **Embracing Change:** *Letting go of past regrets or discontent to move forward positively.*

The "Four of Chalices" card is a depiction of confronting inner discontent and the journey towards understanding and accepting divine grace and mercy. It emphasizes the importance of introspection in overcoming apathy and the potential for a renewed perspective that can lead to gratitude and acceptance of life's offerings.

Five of Chalices

THE PRODIGAL SON

After he had spent all he had,
a severe famine swept through that country,
and he began to be in need.
Luke 15:14 BSB

"After he had spent everything,
there was a severe famine in that whole country,
and he began to be in need."
Luke 15:14 (NIV)

FIVE *of* CHALICES
THE PRODIGAL SON

The parable of the Prodigal Son tells of a young man who asks for his inheritance early, then squanders his wealth in a foreign land, leading to destitution. Upon hitting rock bottom, he decides to return to his father, expecting to be treated as a servant. To his surprise, his father welcomes him with open arms, celebrating his return as if he were dead and is now alive again. The older brother, who stayed and worked diligently, resents the celebration for the wayward son, highlighting themes of jealousy and the challenge of unconditional love and forgiveness.

UPRIGHT KEYWORDS:	REVERSED KEYWORDS:
Loss	*Forgiveness*
Regret	*Moving on*
Sorrow	*Acceptance*
Focusing on the negative	*Finding hope*
Overlooked blessings	*Focusing on the positive*

CARD MEANING IN UPRIGHT POSITION:

Focusing on loss and disappointment, potentially overshadowing the opportunities for healing and redemption that are still available. It signifies a time of sorrow but also hints at the possibility of reconciliation.

- **Loss:** *Experiencing the pain of losing something or someone.*
- **Regret:** *Reflecting on mistakes and wishing for change.*
- **Sorrow:** *Feeling deep sadness over what has been lost.*
- **Focusing on the Negative:** *Overlooking the potential for joy and reconciliation.*
- **Overlooked Blessings:** *Ignoring the possibilities that remain.*

CARD MEANING IN REVERSED POSITION:

A shift in perspective from dwelling on the past to recognizing and appreciating what remains. It is the beginning of forgiveness, healing, and the return to joy.

- **Forgiveness:** *Offering and accepting forgiveness to heal from past hurts.*
- **Moving On:** *Shifting focus from what's been lost to what can be gained.*
- **Acceptance:** *Acknowledging and accepting the past.*
- **Finding Hope:** *Rediscovering optimism and the potential for happiness.*
- **Focusing on the Positive:** *Embracing the good that exists and can be rebuilt.*

The "Five of Chalices" card is a representation of loss and redemption, emphasizing the importance of facing our regrets and sorrows, yet finding the courage to seek forgiveness and embrace the love and opportunities that await. It shows the dual nature of grief: the pain of what we have lost and the hope for what might still be recovered or discovered anew.

Six of Chalices

JESUS AND THE CHILDREN

But when Jesus saw this, He was indignant and told them,
"Let the little children come to Me, and do not hinder them!
For the kingdom of God belongs to such as these.
Mark 10:14 BSB

In Mark 10:13-16, people bring children to Jesus, but the disciples rebuke them. Jesus, displeased, tells the disciples to let the children come to Him and not to hinder them, for the kingdom of God belongs to such as these. He then blesses the children. This moment underscores the value Jesus places on the qualities of children, such as innocence and trust, as essential for entering the kingdom of God.

UPRIGHT KEYWORDS:	REVERSED KEYWORDS:
Innocence	*Stuck in the past*
Nostalgia	*Naivety*
Childhood memories	*Unrealistic expectations*
Joy	*Growing pains*
Simplicity	

CARD MEANING IN UPRIGHT POSITION:

Reflection on past joys and the simplicity of life, suggesting a return to innocence or the comfort of familiar, happy memories. It portrays embracing purity, joy, and the straightforward truths that come from a childlike perspective.

- **Innocence:** *Embracing purity and simplicity in one's approach to life.*
- **Nostalgia:** *Reflecting fondly on past memories and experiences.*
- **Childhood Memories:** *Reconnecting with the joy and wonder of one's early years.*
- **Joy:** *Experiencing genuine happiness and contentment.*
- **Simplicity:** *Appreciating the simple pleasures of life.*

CARD MEANING IN REVERSED POSITION:

Indicates being overly anchored in the past, perhaps idealizing childhood or simpler times to the detriment of present growth. It hints to a need to reconcile with one's past and embrace maturity while retaining the positive aspects of innocence and faith.

- **Stuck in the Past:** *Unable to move forward due to idealization of earlier times.*
- **Naivety:** *Holding onto unrealistic views or expectations based on a simpler past.*
- **Unrealistic Expectations:** *Yearning for a return to a past that cannot be recaptured.*
- **Growing Pains:** *Struggling with the transition from innocence to experience and maturity.*

The "Six of Chalices" underscores themes of embracing the qualities of childhood as a path to spiritual fulfillment, emphasizing innocence, joy, and simplicity. It is essential to maintain a pure heart and the value of childlike faith and wonder in our journey through life, while also recognizing the need to grow and adapt without losing our core essence.

Seven of Chalices

THE TEMPTATION OF CHRIST

*He said to him, "I will give you all of these things,
if you will fall down and worship me."*
Matthew 4:9 WEB

*" 'All this I will give you,' he said,
'if you will bow down and worship me.' "*
Matthew 4:9 (NIV)

SEVEN of CHALICES
THE TEMPTATION OF CHRIST

After fasting for 40 days and nights in the wilderness, Jesus is tempted by the devil. First, Satan tempts Him to turn stones into bread, challenging His hunger. Next, he challenges Jesus to throw Himself down from the pinnacle of the temple in Jerusalem, questioning God's protection. Finally, Satan offers all the kingdoms of the world in exchange for worship. Jesus rebuffs each temptation with scripture, emphasizing reliance on God and adherence to spiritual truth over earthly power or physical needs.

UPRIGHT KEYWORDS:	REVERSED KEYWORDS:
Choices	Clarity
Illusions	Decision
Temptation	Reality
Discernment	Wisdom
Fantasy	Overcoming temptation

CARD MEANING IN UPRIGHT POSITION:

It stands for being confronted with numerous options, some of which may be illusions or distractions from one's true path. It signifies the challenge of discerning between what is real and valuable and what is mere fantasy or temptation.

- **Choices:** *Facing a range of options or paths, requiring careful consideration.*
- **Illusions:** *Being tempted by seemingly attractive options that may lead astray.*
- **Temptation:** *The allure of taking the easier, potentially morally compromising path.*
- **Discernment:** *The need to see beyond illusions and choose wisely.*
- **Fantasy:** *The risk of being caught up in wishful thinking or unrealistic expectations.*

CARD MEANING IN REVERSED POSITION:

Gaining clarity and making a decisive choice among many options. It implies moving past confusion and illusion to embrace reality and act with wisdom.

- **Clarity:** *Gaining a clear understanding of the situation and seeing through deceptions.*
- **Decision:** *Making a definitive choice based on truth and integrity.*
- **Wisdom:** *Applying spiritual or moral principles to overcome challenges.*
- **Overcoming Temptation:** *Resisting distractions and focusing on what is truly important.*

The "Seven of Chalices" is all about being tested, emphasizing the essence of wisdom and discernment in the face of life's illusions and temptations. It underlines the value of making choices grounded in spiritual truth, the strength found in faith, and the clarity that comes from facing reality with integrity.

Eight of Chalices
THE ASCENSION OF JESUS

After He had said this, they watched as He was taken up,
and a cloud hid Him from their sight.
Acts 1:9 BSB

"*After he said this, he was taken up before their very eyes, and a cloud hid him from their sight.*"
Acts 1:9 (NIV)

EIGHT *of* CHALICES
THE ASCENSION OF JESUS

After His resurrection, Jesus appears to His disciples, teaching them about the kingdom of God. At the Mount of Olives, as He blesses them, He is taken up into heaven in their sight, ascending to His Father and signaling the end of His earthly ministry. The disciples are then told by two angels that Jesus will return in the same way He was taken up. This moment of ascension marks a pivotal point for the disciples, urging them to embrace their mission with faith and courage, despite the physical absence of Jesus.

UPRIGHT KEYWORDS:	REVERSED KEYWORDS:
Transition	*Stagnation*
Moving on	*Reluctance to change*
Seeking deeper meaning	*Fear of the unknown*
Letting go	*Unfinished business*

CARD MEANING IN UPRIGHT POSITION:

Embracing change, letting go of the past, and pursuing a path that promises greater spiritual fulfillment, even if it means leaving comfort zones behind.

- **Transition:** *Embracing change and the journey toward spiritual growth.*
- **Moving On:** *Letting go of previous attachments or conditions to seek a higher purpose.*
- **Seeking Deeper Meaning:** *Pursuing a path that offers greater spiritual fulfillment.*
- **Letting Go:** *Releasing what no longer serves in favor of pursuing one's true calling.*

CARD MEANING IN REVERSED POSITION:

Hesitancy to move forward, clinging to the past, or a reluctance to embark on a new spiritual journey due to fear of loss or the unknown.

- **Stagnation:** *Experiencing a lack of progress due to fear or reluctance to change.*
- **Reluctance to Change:** *Holding onto the past or what is familiar at the expense of growth.*
- **Fear of the Unknown:** *Allowing uncertainty to prevent taking the necessary steps forward.*
- **Unfinished Business:** *Feeling unresolved issues or commitments are hindering progress.*

The "Eight of Chalices" card Illustrates the quest for higher understanding. It highlights the journey of moving beyond the known to embrace a deeper, more fulfilling spiritual path, underscored by the disciples' transition from direct companionship with Jesus to a relationship of faith, guided by the Holy Spirit. It emphasizes the crucial role of faith and the courage to seek beyond the visible, trusting in the promise of spiritual presence and guidance.

Nine of Chalices

THE FEAST OF PURIM

...as the days on which the Jews gained rest from their enemies and the month in which their sorrow turned to joy and their mourning into a holiday. He wrote that these were to be days of feasting and joy, of sending gifts to one another and to the poor.
Esther 9:22 BSB

"as the time when the Jews got relief from their enemies, and as the month when their sorrow was turned into joy and their mourning into a day of celebration."
Esther 9:22 (NIV)

NINE of CHALICES
THE FEAST OF PURIM

The story centers around Esther, a Jewish queen of Persia, and her cousin Mordecai, who uncover a plot by Haman, the king's advisor, to annihilate the Jewish people. Through courage, strategic planning, and Esther's intervention with the king, Haman's plans are thwarted. Haman is executed, and the king grants the Jews the right to defend themselves against their enemies. The victory is so complete that it initiates the annual celebration of Purim, marked by feasting, joy, and the exchange of gifts, as a memorial to their deliverance.

UPRIGHT KEYWORDS:	REVERSED KEYWORDS:
Contentment	*Discontent*
Satisfaction	*Greed*
Gratitude	*Smugness*
Joy	*Unfulfilled wishes*
Fulfillment	*Overindulgence*

CARD MEANING IN UPRIGHT POSITION:

Happiness, wish fulfillment, and enjoying the rewards of one's efforts. A period of emotional and possibly material satisfaction, where one feels content with what they have achieved.

- **Satisfaction:** *Enjoying the fruits of one's labor, feeling that desires have been met.*
- **Gratitude:** *Thankfulness for blessings received.*
- **Joy:** *Experiencing great happiness and delight, especially from personal achievements or communal victories.*
- **Fulfillment:** *The sense of having one's wishes or needs met, leading to a state of completeness.*

CARD MEANING IN REVERSED POSITION:

Dissatisfaction despite achievements, possibly due to greed or because the desires fulfilled did not bring the expected happiness. It can also mean overindulgence or taking one's blessings for granted.

- **Discontent:** *Experiencing dissatisfaction with one's achievements, feeling something is still missing.*
- **Greed:** *Wanting more than what one has.*
- **Smugness:** *Exhibiting an excessive pride in one's achievements, which can alienate others.*
- **Unfulfilled Wishes:** *The realization that what was desired does not bring the expected joy or fulfillment.*
- **Overindulgence:** *Excess in celebration or consumption, which can lead to negative consequences.*

The "Nine of Cups" shows collective joy, satisfaction, and the fulfillment of a community's deepest wishes for safety and peace. It emphasizes the value of gratitude and the joy found in shared victories, while also cautioning against the potential pitfalls of complacency, overindulgence, and the belief that external achievements alone can bring true happiness.

Ten of Chalices

ELIZABETH AND ZECHARIAH'S JOY

He will be a joy and delight to you,
and many will rejoice at his birth,
Luke 1:14 BSB

"He will be a joy and delight to you,
and many will rejoice because of his birth"
Luke 1:14 (NIV)

TEN *of* CHALICES
ELIZABETH AND ZECHARIAH'S JOY

Elizabeth and Zechariah, though righteous and blameless before God, were without children because Elizabeth was barren. Zechariah, a priest, encounters an angel while serving in the temple, who tells him they will have a son named John, who will be great before the Lord. Zechariah doubts the angel, and he is rendered mute until the prophecy is fulfilled. Elizabeth conceives, recognizing the child as a blessing from God. Upon John's birth and Zechariah's affirmation of his name, Zechariah's speech is restored, and they are filled with joy and the Holy Spirit, praising God for His mercy and fulfillment of His promises.

UPRIGHT KEYWORDS:	REVERSED KEYWORDS:
Fulfillment	*Disrupted harmony*
Harmony	*Discontent*
Family bliss	*Broken relationships*
Emotional contentment	*Unfulfilled desires*
Gratitude	*Emotional isolation*

CARD MEANING IN UPRIGHT POSITION:

Emotional fulfillment and happiness, particularly within the family or community setting. It symbolizes the joy that comes from harmonious relationships, shared love, and the realization of dreams.

- **Fulfillment:** *Experiencing a profound sense of satisfaction and accomplishment.*
- **Harmony:** *Living in peace and harmony within one's family or community.*
- **Family Bliss:** *Enjoying a period of joy and happiness with loved ones.*
- **Gratitude:** *Expressing thankfulness for life's blessings and the joy they bring.*

CARD MEANING IN REVERSED POSITION:

Discontent or lack of fulfillment in one's personal life or relationships. It draw the attention to issues within the family dynamic or a sense of isolation from loved ones.

- **Disrupted Harmony:** *Encountering conflict or discord within personal relationships.*
- **Discontent:** *Feeling unfulfilled or unhappy despite outward appearances of success.*
- **Broken Relationships:** *Experiencing separation or estrangement from loved ones.*
- **Unfulfilled Desires:** *Yearning for something more or different from what one has.*
- **Emotional Isolation:** *Feeling disconnected from family or community support.*

The "Ten of Cups" card is a narrative of divine blessings, familial happiness, and the profound joy that comes from answered prayers and fulfilled desires. It point out the true emotional fulfillment found in family and community, underscoring the value of gratitude and the beauty of life's miraculous moments, while also acknowledging the challenges that can disrupt this ideal harmony.

Page of Chalices

SAMUEL, THE BOY PROPHET

Then the LORD came and stood there, calling as before,
"Samuel! Samuel!" And Samuel answered,
"Speak, for Your servant is listening."
1 Samuel 3:10 BSB

The story of Samuel begins with his mother, Hannah, praying for a child and promising to dedicate him to God's service. Samuel is born and, true to her word, Hannah brings him to serve under Eli, the priest, at the temple. One night, God calls to Samuel, and with Eli's guidance, Samuel responds, "Speak, for your servant is listening." This marks the beginning of Samuel's journey as a prophet, chosen by God to deliver messages to Israel. Samuel grows up to be a respected prophet, known for his integrity and his role in anointing the first two kings of Israel, Saul and David.

"The Lord came and stood there, calling as at the other times, 'Samuel! Samuel!' Then Samuel said, 'Speak, for your servant is listening.' "
1 Samuel 3:10 (NIV)

PAGE of CHALICES
SAMUEL, THE BOY PROPHET

UPRIGHT KEYWORDS:	REVERSED KEYWORDS:
Intuition	*Emotional immaturity*
Emotional curiosity	*Ignoring intuition*
Innocence	*Disappointment*
A message	*Inward-focused*
Spiritual insight	*Missed opportunities*

CARD MEANING IN UPRIGHT POSITION:

Emotional and spiritual exploration, being open to messages from the subconscious or the divine. It symbolizes the beginnings of understanding one's emotional and intuitive landscape.

- **Intuition:** *Trusting in and listening to one's inner voice.*
- **Emotional Curiosity:** *Exploring one's feelings with openness and innocence.*
- **Innocence:** *Approaching life with a pure heart and genuine intentions.*
- **A Message:** *Receiving important emotional or spiritual insights.*
- **Beginnings of Spiritual Insight:** *The initial steps on a journey of deeper understanding and connection.*

CARD MEANING IN REVERSED POSITION:

Ignoring the inner voice or emotional truths, leading to a sense of unfulfillment or missed spiritual opportunities. It implies a need to reconnect with one's intuition and feelings.

- **Emotional Immaturity:** *Struggling to understand or deal with one's emotions effectively.*
- **Ignoring Intuition:** *Overlooking the significance of one's inner voice or feelings.*
- **Inward-focused:** *Being overly self-absorbed, missing the chance to connect more deeply with others or the divine.*
- **Missed Emotional Opportunities:** *Failing to embrace chances for emotional growth or spiritual insight.*

The "Page of Chalices" illustrates youthful openness to the divine and the purity of responding to one's calling with a whole heart. It focuses on the power of listening to and trusting in both divine and inner guidance, reflecting on the journey of discovering one's spiritual and emotional paths, and the joy and challenges found in embracing such insights.

Knight of Chalices

YOUNG DAVID

And whenever the spirit from God came upon Saul, David would pick up his harp and play. Then Saul would find relief and feel better, and the spirit of distress would depart from him.
1 Samuel 16:23 BSB

"Whenever the spirit from God came on Saul,
David would take up his lyre and play.
Then relief would come to Saul; he would feel better,
and the evil spirit would leave him."
1 Samuel 16:23 (NIV)

KNIGHT *of* CHALICES
YOUNG DAVID

When David is brought to Saul's court for the first time. Saul is tormented by an evil spirit, and it is suggested that a skilled harpist might soothe him. David, known both for his bravery and his musical talent, is summoned to play the lyre for Saul. David's music successfully calms Saul, driving the evil spirit away and bringing peace to the troubled king. This episode showcases David's gentle, compassionate side and his ability to bring healing and comfort through his artistry and presence.

UPRIGHT KEYWORDS:	REVERSED KEYWORDS:
Emotional healing	*Emotional manipulation*
Artistic expression	*Over-sensitivity*
Gentleness	*Moodiness*
Sensitivity	*Disconnection*
Peacemaker	*Escapism through art*

CARD MEANING IN UPRIGHT POSITION:

Symbolizes the journey of using one's talents and sensitivity to bring peace and emotional well-being to oneself and others. It represents the healing potential of art and the importance of approaching situations with kindness and empathy.

- **Emotional Healing:** *Using compassion and sensitivity to heal wounds.*
- **Artistic Expression:** *Conveying emotions through art.*
- **Gentleness:** *Approaching situations with kindness.*
- **Sensitivity:** *Being attuned to the emotional states of oneself and others.*
- **Peacemaker:** *Acting as a conduit for harmony and understanding.*

CARD MEANING IN REVERSED POSITION:

A situation where emotional sensitivity may lead to vulnerability or where talents are used to escape reality rather than confront it. It shows a need for grounding and connecting more authentically with one's emotions.

- **Emotional Manipulation:** *Misusing one's emotional insight for personal gain.*
- **Over-sensitivity:** *Allowing emotions to overwhelm and dictate actions.*
- **Moodiness:** *Being caught in the sway of fluctuating emotions.*
- **Disconnection from One's Feelings:** *Struggling to engage authentically with inner emotions.*

The "Knight of Chalices" shows Young David's role as a healer and peacemaker through his emotional depth and artistic talent. It demonstrates the transformative power of empathy, art, and gentleness, while also cautioning against the potential shadows of emotional sensitivity, such as disconnection or escapism.

Queen of Chalices

HANNAH - MOTHER OF FAITH

*I prayed for this boy, and since the LORD has granted me what I
asked of Him, I now dedicate the boy to the LORD.
For as long as he lives, he is dedicated to the LORD."*
1 Samuel 1:27-28 BSB

*"I prayed for this child, and the Lord has granted me
what I asked of him. So now I give him to the Lord.
For his whole life he will be given over to the Lord."*
1 Samuel 1:27-28 (NIV)

QUEEN of CHALICES
HANNAH - MOTHER OF FAITH

Hannah, deeply distressed by her inability to bear children, prays fervently to God at the temple in Shiloh, promising that if He gives her a son, she will dedicate him to the Lord's service. Eli, the priest, initially mistakes her silent prayers for drunkenness, but upon understanding her sincerity, blesses her wish. God hears Hannah's prayers, and she conceives Samuel, whom she later brings to the temple to serve God, fulfilling her vow. Hannah's story is a poignant testament to faith, perseverance, and the profound bond between mother and child.

UPRIGHT KEYWORDS:	REVERSED KEYWORDS:
Deep empathy	Emotional dependency
Intuition	Overwhelmed by sorrow
Unconditional love	Neglect
Emotional strength	Moodiness
Nurturing	Smothering care

CARD MEANING IN UPRIGHT POSITION:

Compassion, understanding, and emotional depth. It signifies the ability to connect with and heal others through empathy and love, and the strength to remain faithful and hopeful through emotional trials.

- **Deep Empathy:** *Connecting with others on an emotional level, understanding their pain and joy.*
- **Intuition:** *Trusting one's inner guidance and perceptions.*
- **Unconditional Love:** *Loving others without expectation, as Hannah loved Samuel.*
- **Emotional Strength:** *Demonstrating resilience in the face of personal pain.*
- **Nurturing:** *Providing care and encouragement, fostering growth in others.*

CARD MEANING IN REVERSED POSITION:

Indicates being consumed by one's emotions or the challenges of care-giving, potentially leading to neglect of one's needs or the imposition of one's emotions onto others. It draws attention to finding a balance between caring for others and self-care.

- **Emotional Dependency:** *Relying too heavily on others for emotional support.*
- **Overwhelmed by Sorrow:** *Allowing grief or sadness to dominate one's life.*
- **Moodiness:** *Being subject to fluctuating emotions that affect those around you.*
- **Smothering Care:** *Offering love and support to the point of stifling independence.*

The "Queen of Chalices" is an instance of profound faith, emotional depth, and the journey from sorrow to fulfillment through the power of prayer and love. It emphasizes the strength found in vulnerability, while also highlighting the importance of balancing emotional giving with self-care and awareness.

King of Chalices

NEHEMIAH REBUILDING JERUSALEM

"You see the trouble we are in. Jerusalem lies in ruins, and its gates have been burned down. Come, let us rebuild the wall of Jerusalem, so that we will no longer be a disgrace."
Nehemiah 2:17 BSB

Nehemiah, serving as the cupbearer to the Persian king Artaxerxes, learns of the desolation of Jerusalem and its walls. Moved by this news, he prays to God and seeks the king's permission to rebuild Jerusalem. Granted authority and resources, Nehemiah travels to Jerusalem and organizes the reconstruction efforts, overcoming obstacles such as local opposition and the demoralization of the Jewish people. Through his leadership, the walls are rebuilt, symbolizing the restoration of the community's safety and spirit.

UPRIGHT KEYWORDS:	REVERSED KEYWORDS:
Compassionate leadership	*Emotional manipulation*
Emotional stability	*Withdrawn*
Diplomacy	*Overbearing*
Wisdom	*Aloofness*
Supportive	*Indecisiveness*

CARD MEANING IN UPRIGHT POSITION:

Symbolizes a figure who leads with emotional depth and understanding, leveraging wisdom and diplomacy to navigate and resolve challenges. This leader supports and uplifts others, fostering unity and resilience.

- **Compassionate Leadership:** *Guiding others with a deep understanding and empathy.*
- **Emotional Stability:** *Maintaining calm and composed in the face of adversity.*
- **Diplomacy:** *Using tact to overcome obstacles.*
- **Wisdom:** *Applying insight and experience to make informed decisions.*
- **Supportive:** *Providing encouragement and support to foster community strength.*

CARD MEANING IN REVERSED POSITION:

Potential misuse of emotional insight for personal gain, or a leader who may become disconnected from the emotional needs of those they lead, leading to indecision or a lack of genuine support.

- **Emotional Manipulation:** *Leveraging emotional understanding for selfish ends.*
- **Withdrawn:** *Becoming detached from the needs and feelings of others.*
- **Overbearing:** *Dominating rather than guiding, stifling community input.*
- **Indecisiveness:** *Failing to make decisions due to emotional turmoil or disconnection.*

The "King of Chalices" card is a representation of nurturing and strategic leadership, showcasing the power of emotional intelligence and compassion in achieving collective goals. It focuses on the balance between strength and sensitivity, highlighting the importance of a leader who is both emotionally aware and decisively action-oriented.

MINOR ARCANA

Feathers

Ace of Feathers

SAUL'S CONVERSION

He fell to the ground and heard a voice say to him,
"Saul, Saul, why do you persecute Me?"
Acts 9:4 BSB

"He fell to the ground and heard a voice say to him,
'Saul, Saul, why do you persecute me?'"
Acts 9:4 (NIV)

ACE *of* FEATHERS
SAUL'S CONVERSION

Saul, known for persecuting early Christians, experiences a divine intervention while on his way to Damascus to arrest more followers of Jesus. A blinding light from heaven strikes him down, and he hears the voice of Jesus asking, "Saul, Saul, why do you persecute me?" Temporarily blinded, Saul is led into Damascus, where Ananias, a disciple, is instructed by God to heal him. Saul's sight is restored, he is baptized, and filled with the Holy Spirit. He begins to preach that Jesus is the Son of God, marking a complete transformation from persecutor to apostle, and becomes known as Paul.

UPRIGHT KEYWORDS:	REVERSED KEYWORDS:
Mental clarity	*Confusion*
Breakthrough	*Misuse of power*
Truth	*Miscommunication*
Justice	*Overwhelm*
Transformation	*Brutality*

CARD MEANING IN UPRIGHT POSITION:

A profound insight or realization that brings about a radical change in perspective or behavior. It signifies the emergence of truth and justice, and the power of intellectual clarity to transform one's life path.

- **Mental Clarity:** *Gaining a clear understanding or insight that changes one's direction.*
- **Breakthrough:** *Experiencing a significant realization that leads to a new way of thinking.*
- **Truth:** *Embracing a new, transformative truth that alters one's life and beliefs.*
- **Transformation:** *Undergoing a profound change in identity, purpose, or belief system.*

CARD MEANING IN REVERSED POSITION:

Confusion, miscommunication, or the negative consequences of using intellectual power to harm others. It suggests a need to reassess one's thoughts to avoid misunderstanding and conflict.

- **Confusion:** *Struggling with unclear thinking or uncertainty about one's beliefs.*
- **Misuse of Power:** *Using intellectual or communicative power to dominate or harm.*
- **Miscommunication:** *Experiencing misunderstandings or failing to convey one's true intentions.*
- **Overwhelm:** *Feeling inundated by too many ideas or too much information.*
- **Brutality:** *The potential for harshness or cruelty in words or thoughts.*

The "Ace of Feathers" shows dramatic insight and transformation. It highlights the sudden clarity and truth that can alter one's course, embodying the dual nature of the mind and communication as tools for both significant change and challenge.

Two of Feathers

GOD TESTS ABRAHAM'S FAITH

"Take your son," God said, "your only son Isaac, whom you love, and go to the land of Moriah. Offer him there as a burnt offering on one of the mountains, which I will show you."
Genesis 22:2 BSB

God tests Abraham's faith by asking him to sacrifice his son Isaac as a burnt offering. Despite the unimaginable emotional turmoil this request causes, Abraham prepares to obey God's command. However, as Abraham raises his knife, an angel of the Lord intervenes, stopping him and providing a ram as an alternative sacrifice. This test demonstrates Abraham's unwavering faith and obedience to God, and it reinforces the covenant between God and Abraham's descendants.

UPRIGHT KEYWORDS:	REVERSED KEYWORDS:
Difficult decisions	*Indecision*
Crossroads	*Avoidance*
Stalemate	*Confusion*
Balance	*Release of tension*
Faith under pressure	*Overwhelmed by emotions*

CARD MEANING IN UPRIGHT POSITION:

A moment of indecision or deadlock where a critical choice must be made, often involving conflicting emotions or values. It constitute the need for clarity and resolution in the face of a challenging dilemma.

- **Difficult Decisions:** *Facing a choice that tests one's values or beliefs.*
- **Crossroads:** *Standing at a pivotal point, needing to choose a path forward.*
- **Stalemate:** *Experiencing a deadlock where neither option seems ideal.*
- **Balance:** *Seeking equilibrium between competing forces.*
- **Faith under Pressure:** *Maintaining belief and integrity in challenging circumstances.*

CARD MEANING IN REVERSED POSITION:

Avoidance of making a necessary choice. It implies confusion, the potential for missed opportunities due to indecisiveness, or the overwhelming influence of emotions on decision-making.

- **Indecision:** *Struggling to make a choice*
- **Avoidance:** *Dodging a difficult decision, potentially causing more issues.*
- **Confusion:** *Feeling uncertain about the correct course of action.*
- **Release of Tension:** *Finding relief from a difficult decision, whether through action or circumstance.*
- **Overwhelmed by Emotions:** *Allowing feelings to cloud judgment, complicating the decision-making process.*

The "Two of Feathers" describes profound moral and emotional dilemma, focusing on the tension between duty and love, and the faith required to navigate such trials. It emphasizes the need to align emotional and rational aspects in decision-making, and the part faith plays in directing these essential choices.

Three of Feathers

BETRAYAL OF A SON

The king was shaken and went up to the chamber over the gate and wept. And as he walked, he cried out, "O my son Absalom! My son, my son Absalom! If only I had died instead of you, O Absalom, my son, my son!"
2 Samuel 18:33 BSB

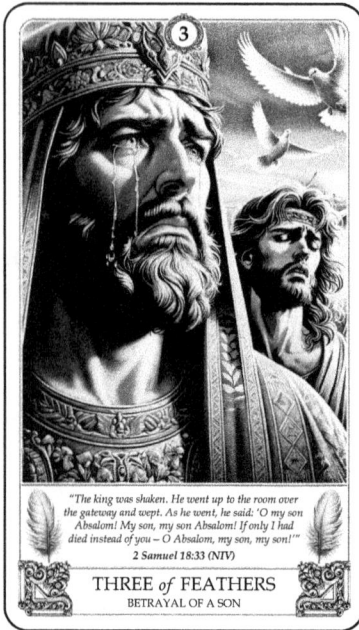

"The king was shaken. He went up to the room over the gateway and wept. As he went, he said: 'O my son Absalom! My son, my son Absalom! If only I had died instead of you – O Absalom, my son, my son!'"
2 Samuel 18:33 (NIV)

THREE *of* FEATHERS
BETRAYAL OF A SON

Absalom, King David's son, rebels against his father in an attempt to usurp the throne, leading to civil war in Israel. Despite the betrayal and conflict, David orders his generals to deal gently with Absalom. However, in the heat of battle, Absalom is killed. When David hears of his son's death, he is overwhelmed with grief, mourning deeply for Absalom and wishing he had died in his son's place. This moment underscores the profound pain of personal loss and the heartache stemming from family conflict and betrayal.

UPRIGHT KEYWORDS:	REVERSED KEYWORDS:
Heartbreak	Healing
Betrayal	Release
Loss	Forgiveness
Sorrow	Overcoming grief
Separation	Reconciliation

CARD MEANING IN UPRIGHT POSITION:

Experiencing of emotional pain due to loss, betrayal, or a difficult separation. It symbolizes the need to confront and process one's sorrow to begin the healing journey.

- **Heartbreak:** *Experiencing profound sadness due to betrayal or loss.*
- **Betrayal:** *Feeling the sting of trust broken, especially by someone close.*
- **Loss:** *Mourning the absence of a loved one or the end of a relationship.*
- **Sorrow:** *Navigating the depths of grief and pain.*
- **Separation:** *Dealing with the fallout of relationships torn apart by conflict.*

CARD MEANING IN REVERSED POSITION:

Recovery from heartbreak, the process of healing wounds, and the possibility of moving past grief and towards forgiveness and reconciliation.

- **Healing:** *Beginning to recover from emotional wounds and finding peace.*
- **Release:** *Letting go and moving forward with one's life.*
- **Forgiveness:** *Choosing to forgive those who have caused pain, whether they are others or oneself.*
- **Overcoming Grief:** *Gradually overcoming the intense sorrow of loss.*
- **Reconciliation:** *The potential to mend relationships and rebuild connections.*

The "Three of Feathers" card is an instance of deep emotional pain rooted in familial conflict and loss. This card shines the spotlight on the universal experiences of heartbreak and sorrow that come from betrayal and loss, while also pointing to the potential for healing, forgiveness, and eventual reconciliation, reflecting the complex nature of human emotions and relationships.

Four of Feathers

ELIJAH'S RETREAT INTO SILENCE

After the earthquake there was a fire, but the LORD was not in the fire. And after the fire came a still, small voice.
1 Kings 19:12 BSB

"After the earthquake came a fire, but the Lord was not in the fire. And after the fire came a gentle whisper."
1 Kings 19:12 (NIV)

FOUR *of* FEATHERS
ELIJAH'S RETREAT INTO SILENCE

After a significant victory at Mount Carmel, where Elijah demonstrates God's power over the prophets of Baal, Jezebel threatens Elijah's life, causing him to flee into the wilderness. Feeling defeated and isolated, Elijah seeks refuge in a cave on Mount Horeb. There God speaks to Elijah in a "gentle whisper," providing him with guidance, comfort, and the strength to continue his prophetic mission. This moment of quiet reflection and divine encounter highlights the importance of solitude and rest for spiritual clarity and renewal.

UPRIGHT KEYWORDS:	REVERSED KEYWORDS:
Rest	*Restlessness*
Contemplation	*Isolation*
Recovery	*Stagnation*
Solitude	*Exhaustion*
Preparation	*Ignoring warnings*

CARD MEANING IN UPRIGHT POSITION:

A necessary pause for rest, reflection, and rejuvenation. It represents a time to recuperate from life's battles and to seek inner peace and guidance before moving forward.

- **Rest:** *Taking a necessary break to restore one's mental, physical, and spiritual energy.*
- **Contemplation:** *Reflecting deeply on one's life path, choices, and the divine will.*
- **Recovery:** *Healing from stress or exhaustion.*
- **Solitude:** *Seeking solitude to better listen to one's inner voice and divine guidance.*
- **Preparation:** *A period of rest to prepare for future challenges and decisions.*

CARD MEANING IN REVERSED POSITION:

Restlessness or isolation that may be detrimental, or a warning against neglecting one's need for a pause. It warns about the potential negative effects of avoiding rest or reflection.

- **Restlessness:** *Feeling unable to relax or pause, possibly due to anxiety or fear.*
- **Isolation:** *Experiencing loneliness or isolation that hinders rather than heals.*
- **Stagnation:** *Staying in a place of rest too long, leading to stagnation or apathy.*
- **Exhaustion:** *Ignoring the body's and mind's needs for rest, leading to burnout.*
- **Ignoring Warnings:** *Overlooking the need for recovery and the signs to slow down..*

The "Four of Feathers" is an example of seeking solace and clarity through withdrawal and rest. It conveys the vital role of rest and contemplation in overcoming adversity, the power of silence for receiving divine guidance, and the importance of preparing oneself spiritually and mentally before facing the world again.

Five of Feathers

KING SAUL'S TRAGIC DOWNFALL

The LORD has torn the kingdom out of your hand
and given it to your neighbor David.
1 Samuel 28:17 BSB

"The Lord has torn the kingdom out of your hands
and given it to one of your neighbors – to David."
1 Samuel 28:17 (NIV)

FIVE *of* FEATHERS
KING SAUL'S TRAGIC DOWNFALL

King Saul, the first king of Israel, initially chosen by God to lead, faces a tragic downfall due to a series of disobediences and moral failures. One pivotal moment comes when God commands Saul through Samuel to destroy the Amalekites completely as divine retribution for their opposition to Israel. Saul, however, spares the king of the Amalekites, and the best of their livestock. Samuel confronts Saul and announces God's rejection of Saul as king. This event marks the beginning of Saul's decline, highlighting the dangers of disobedience, pride, and the prioritization of personal desires over divine commands.

UPRIGHT KEYWORDS:	REVERSED KEYWORDS:
Conflict	*Reconciliation*
Defeat	*Learning from mistakes*
Consequences	*Letting go of conflict*
Hollow victory	*Making amends*
Loss	*Moving forward*

CARD MEANING IN UPRIGHT POSITION:

Situations of conflict and the aftermath of questionable decisions. It exemplifies the fallout of acting in self-interest, leading to loss and regret.

- **Conflict:** *Engaging in actions that lead to strife and discord.*
- **Defeat:** *Experiencing the repercussions of one's actions, leading to a sense of loss.*
- **Consequences:** *Facing the negative outcomes of decisions made in self-interest.*
- **Hollow Victory:** *Winning at a cost that negates the value of the victory itself.*
- **Loss:** *Realizing the true cost of one's actions, leading to sorrow and regret.*

CARD MEANING IN REVERSED POSITION:

Recovery and learning from past mistakes. Potential for moving past conflict, seeking reconciliation, and making amends for previous actions.

- **Reconciliation:** *Seeking to mend relationships and resolve past conflicts.*
- **Learning from Mistakes:** *Gaining insight from previous errors and changing one's course.*
- **Letting Go of Conflict:** *Choosing peace and understanding over continuing strife.*
- **Moving Forward:** *Embracing the lessons learned to proceed with greater wisdom.*

The "Five of Feathers" illustrates the consequences of disobedience and the pursuit of personal agenda over collective well-being. It focuses on the humility and obedience, while also highlighting the potential for growth and redemption through acknowledgment and rectification of past mistakes.

Six of Feathers

RUTH THE MOABITE

"Do not urge me to leave you or to turn from following you.
For wherever you go, I will go, and wherever you live, I will live;
your people will be my people, and your God will be my God.
Ruth 1:16 BSB

> "But Ruth replied, 'Don't urge me to leave you or to turn back from you. Where you go I will go, and where you stay I will stay. Your people will be my people and your God my God.'"
> Ruth 1:16 (NIV)
>
> SIX of FEATHERS
> RUTH THE MOABITE

Following the deaths of her sons, Naomi decides to leave Moab and return to Bethlehem. She urges her daughters-in-law, Orpah and Ruth, to remain in Moab and remarry. Orpah eventually stays, but Ruth clings to Naomi, famously declaring, *"Where you go I will go, and where you stay I will stay. Your people will be my people and your God my God."* Ruth's loyalty leads her to a new land and eventually to marriage with Boaz, a relative of Naomi's husband. Through her faithfulness and resilience, Ruth becomes the great-grandmother of King David, integrating into the lineage of Jesus.

UPRIGHT KEYWORDS:	REVERSED KEYWORDS:
Transition	*Resistance to change*
Healing journey	*Stagnation*
Moving forward	*Unresolved issues*
Seeking a new beginning	*Emotional baggage*
Releasing the past	*Fear of the unknown*

CARD MEANING IN UPRIGHT POSITION:

Moving away from past difficulties towards a hopeful future. It symbolizes the necessity of transitions for growth and healing, acknowledging the challenges of leaving behind the familiar to embrace new opportunities.

- **Transition:** *Embarking on a journey from a place of hardship to one of potential and hope.*
- **Healing Journey:** *Moving towards recovery and emotional healing.*
- **Moving Forward:** *Taking steps to leave behind difficulties and seeking a brighter future.*
- **Seeking a New Beginning:** *Actively looking for opportunities to start afresh.*
- **Releasing the Past:** *Letting go and embracing change.*

CARD MEANING IN REVERSED POSITION:

Reluctance or inability to move on from the past, possibly due to fear, attachment, or unresolved emotional issues. It indicates a need to address what holds one back to truly progress.

- **Resistance to Change:** *Holding on to the past or fearing the transition to new experiences.*
- **Stagnation:** *Discomfort due to indecision or fear.*
- **Unresolved Issues:** *Carrying burdens that need addressing before moving forward.*
- **Emotional Baggage:** *The impact of past experiences on one's ability to embrace the future.*
- **Fear of the Unknown:** *Anxiety about what lies ahead, impeding progress.*

Ruth's journey symbolizes the courage it takes to leave behind the known for the promise of a new beginning, highlighting the healing and growth that can come from such a transition. It is based on faith, both in oneself and in the journey, as a vehicle for overcoming challenges and moving towards a more hopeful future.

Seven of Feathers

JACOB THE DECEIVER

Jacob said to his father, "I am Esau, your firstborn.
I have done as you told me. Please sit up and eat some of my game,
so that you may bless me."
Genesis 27:19 BSB

Isaac, who is old and blind, intends to bless his eldest son Esau, a tradition granting rights and inheritance. Rebekah, overhearing this and favoring Jacob, orchestrates a deceit: Jacob, disguised as Esau, receives Isaac's blessing by pretending to be his brother. When Esau learns of the betrayal, he is devastated, and Jacob must flee to avoid his brother's wrath. This pivotal act of deception shapes much of Jacob's future, teaching profound lessons about truth, consequence, and the complexity of familial bonds.

UPRIGHT KEYWORDS:	REVERSED KEYWORDS:
Strategy	*Exposure*
Deception	*Guilt*
Caution	*Reckoning*
Cunning	*Regret*
Secret plans	*Dishonesty revealed*

CARD MEANING IN UPRIGHT POSITION:

Actions taken with strategic intent, possibly in secret, to advance one's goals. It represents the use of intellect and cunning to navigate challenges, while also hinting at the ethical implications of such strategies.

- **Strategy:** *Employing careful planning to achieve a specific goal.*
- **Deception:** *Using deceit as a tool to gain advantage.*
- **Caution:** *Being wary of the potential fallout from secretive actions.*
- **Cunning:** *Demonstrating cleverness or skill in executing plans.*
- **Secret Plans:** *Concealing one's true intentions or actions.*

CARD MEANING IN REVERSED POSITION:

Deceitful actions coming to light, leading to guilt, regret, and the need to face the repercussions of one's behavior. It suggests a moment of reckoning and the potential for seeking redemption or reconciliation.

- **Exposure:** *Having one's deceit or strategic maneuvers revealed.*
- **Guilt:** *Feeling remorse for actions taken at the expense of others.*
- **Reckoning:** *Facing the consequences of one's actions.*
- **Regret:** *Reflecting on the moral cost of achieving one's goals dishonestly.*
- **Dishonesty Revealed:** *The truth coming to light, prompting a reevaluation of one's actions.*

The "Seven of Feathers" is all about the nuanced balance between cunning strategy and the values of honesty and integrity, as well as the inevitable confrontation with the consequences of one's choices.

Eight of Feathers

JONAH TRAPPED INSIDE THE FISH

"In my distress I called to the LORD, and He answered me. From the belly of Sheol I called for help, and You heard my voice.
Jonah 2:2 BSB

"He said: 'In my distress I called to the Lord, and he answered me. From deep in the realm of the dead I called for help, and you listened to my cry.'"
Jonah 2:2 (NIV)

EIGHT *of* FEATHERS
JONAH TRAPPED INSIDE THE FISH

God commands Jonah to go to Nineveh and preach against its wickedness. Jonah, however, flees in the opposite direction, boarding a ship to Tarshish. A great storm endangers the ship, and Jonah, realizing he is the cause for the storm, asks to be thrown overboard, leading to him being swallowed by a great fish. Inside the fish for three days and nights, Jonah prays to God, repenting for his disobedience. God commands the fish to spit Jonah onto dry land, giving him a second chance to fulfill his mission. This experience transforms Jonah, teaching him about obedience, repentance, and God's mercy.

UPRIGHT KEYWORDS:	**REVERSED KEYWORDS:**
Entrapment	*Liberation*
Self-imposed restrictions	*Self-awareness*
Victim mentality	*Overcoming fears*
Feeling powerless	*Taking responsibility*
Need for perspective shift	*Finding inner strength*

CARD MEANING IN UPRIGHT POSITION:

Feeling trapped, often by one's own beliefs or choices, leading to a sense of powerlessness and the need for a shift in perspective to find a way out.

- **Entrapment:** *Feeling caught in an undesirable situation, often due to avoidance or denial.*
- **Self-imposed Restrictions:** *Limiting oneself through negative beliefs or fear.*
- **Victim Mentality:** *Perceiving oneself as powerless, overlooking avenues for change.*
- **Feeling Powerless:** *A lack of belief in one's ability to alter one's circumstances.*
- **Need for Perspective Shift:** *Recognizing that the key to liberation is changing one's mindset or approach.*

CARD MEANING IN REVERSED POSITION:

A turning point where one recognizes their power to escape their predicament, symbolizing self-awareness, acceptance of responsibility, and the inner strength to overcome challenges.

- **Liberation:** *Breaking free from limitations.*
- **Self-awareness:** *Gaining insight into one's actions and their consequences.*
- **Overcoming Fears:** *Facing and moving beyond fears that have held one back.*
- **Taking Responsibility:** *Realizing one's role in creating the current situation and taking steps to change it.*
- **Finding Inner Strength:** *Discovering the resilience and determination within to overcome obstacles.*

The "Eight of Feathers" encapsulates themes of introspection, constraint, and the journey towards understanding and accepting personal responsibility. It shows the importance of facing the consequences of our actions, the power of repentance, and the liberating realization that we often hold the keys to our own imprisonment.

Nine of Feathers

PETER DENIES JESUS

Then Peter remembered the word that Jesus had spoken:
"Before the rooster crows, you will deny Me three times."
And he went outside and wept bitterly.
Matthew 26:75 BSB

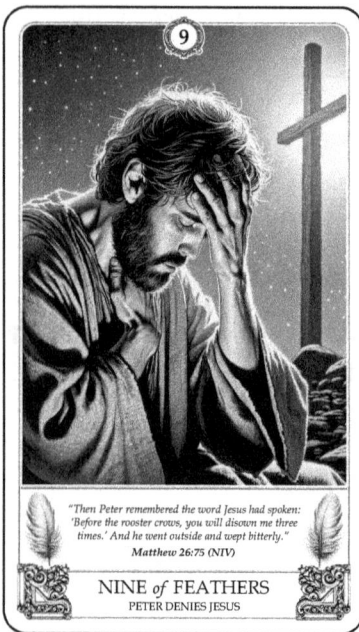

"*Then Peter remembered the word Jesus had spoken:*
'Before the rooster crows, you will disown me three
times.' And he went outside and wept bitterly."
Matthew 26:75 (NIV)

NINE *of* FEATHERS
PETER DENIES JESUS

Before Jesus' crucifixion, He predicts that Peter will deny Him three times before the rooster crows. Despite Peter's initial protestations of loyalty, when confronted by others, Peter denies knowing Jesus to protect himself. After the third denial, the rooster crows, and Peter remembers Jesus' words. Overwhelmed by guilt and shame, Peter weeps bitterly. This event marks a profound moment of personal failure and anguish for Peter, yet it also sets the stage for his later redemption and leadership in the early Christian community.

UPRIGHT KEYWORDS:	REVERSED KEYWORDS:
Guilt	*Overcoming guilt*
Remorse	*Learning from mistakes*
Anxiety	*Release from worry*
Fear of consequences	*Seeking forgiveness*
Mental anguish	*Healing after remorse*

CARD MEANING IN UPRIGHT POSITION:

Deep anxiety, guilt, or mental turmoil, often stemming from one's actions or failures. It emphasizes the weight of conscience and the struggle with inner demons of regret and fear.

- **Guilt:** *Experiencing a profound sense of guilt over actions taken or not taken.*
- **Remorse:** *Feeling deep regret for one's actions, particularly those that betray moral principles.*
- **Anxiety:** *Suffering from anxiety over anticipated consequences or moral dilemmas.*
- **Fear of Consequences:** *Worrying about the fallout from one's actions or decisions.*
- **Mental Anguish:** *Enduring significant emotional distress, often in solitude.*

CARD MEANING IN REVERSED POSITION:

Overcoming one's inner turmoil, finding ways to forgive oneself, and learning from past errors. It shows a path towards healing and the alleviation of mental distress.

- **Overcoming Guilt:** *Starting to move beyond guilt.*
- **Learning from Mistakes:** *Using past errors as lessons for personal growth and better choices.*
- **Release from Worry:** *Gradually freeing oneself from the grip of anxiety and worry.*
- **Seeking Forgiveness:** *Actively pursuing reconciliation, both with oneself and others.*
- **Healing after Remorse:** *Embarking on a path towards emotional and mental recovery.*

The "Nine of Feathers" illustrates the human struggle with guilt and the journey towards redemption and forgiveness. It describes the emotional turmoil following actions that betray one's values or bonds but also points towards the possibility of learning, healing, and ultimately finding peace through acceptance and transformation.

Ten of Feathers

SAMSON LOSES HIS STRENGTH

And having lulled him to sleep on her lap,
she called a man to shave off the seven braids of his head.
In this way she began to subdue him, and his strength left him.
Judges 16:19 BSB

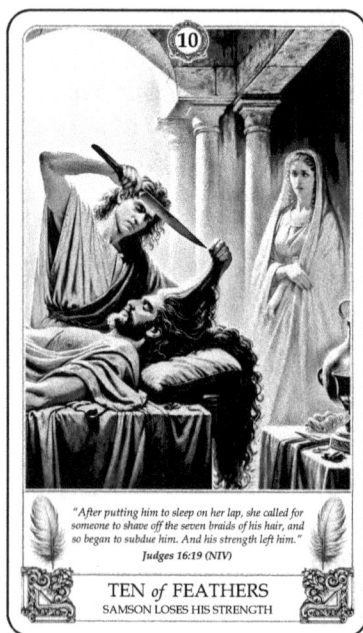

"After putting him to sleep on her lap, she called for someone to shave off the seven braids of his hair, and so began to subdue him. And his strength left him."
Judges 16:19 (NIV)

TEN *of* FEATHERS
SAMSON LOSES HIS STRENGTH

Samson, granted extraordinary strength by God, becomes vulnerable through his love for Delilah. The Philistine rulers bribe Delilah to discover the source of Samson's strength. After three failed attempts, she finally coaxes the secret from him: his uncut hair, a symbol of his vow to God. While he sleeps, Delilah has his hair cut, and Samson's strength leaves him. The Philistines capture, blind, and imprison him. However, in his final act, Samson calls upon God, and his strength is temporarily restored, allowing him to bring down the temple of Dagon, dying, but achieving a posthumous victory.

UPRIGHT KEYWORDS:	REVERSED KEYWORDS:
Betrayal	*Recovery*
Loss	*Hope after despair*
Downfall	*Release from betrayal*
End of a cycle	*Lessons learned*
Victimhood	*Resilience*

CARD MEANING IN UPRIGHT POSITION:

Betrayal or loss, marking a painful but necessary end to a particular phase, often felt as a profound personal defeat. It underscores the need to confront the reality of the situation to move forward.

- **Betrayal:** *Experiencing a profound personal betrayal.*
- **Loss:** *The feeling of having everything taken away, leading to a significant low point.*
- **Downfall:** *The culmination of actions and consequences that lead to one's undoing.*
- **End of a Cycle:** *Marking a definitive end, with all illusions shattered.*
- **Victimhood:** *Feeling powerless and defeated, often by one's own choices or trust in others.*

CARD MEANING IN REVERSED POSITION:

Healing from a significant betrayal or downfall. It represents the finding of inner strength, learning from past experiences, and the slow rebuild towards a brighter future.

- **Recovery:** *Beginning the process of healing and reclaiming lost power or dignity.*
- **Hope after Despair:** *The first signs of emerging from a period of intense difficulty or betrayal.*
- **Release from Betrayal:** *Working through feelings of betrayal to find forgiveness or acceptance.*
- **Lessons Learned:** *Gaining wisdom from the experience and using it to prevent future downfalls.*
- **Resilience:** *Discovering an inner resilience and strength that was previously unacknowledged.*

The "Ten of Feathers" is a testament to the human spirit's ability to endure, learn, and find a way to rise again, even in the face of overwhelming defeat. It emphasizes the duality of human experience — the depths of despair can also be the soil from which new strength and wisdom grow.

Page of Feathers

ESTHER SAVES THE JEWS

Queen Esther replied, "If I have found favor in your sight, O king, and if it pleases the king, grant me my life as my petition, and the lives of my people as my request.
Esther 7:3 BSB

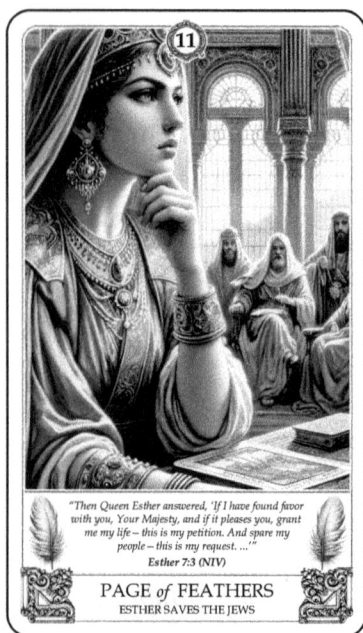

Esther, a Jewish woman who becomes queen of Persia without revealing her ethnicity, discovers a plot by Haman, the king's advisor, to exterminate the Jewish people. Esther courageously plans a banquet for King Ahasuerus and Haman, where she reveals her Jewish identity and exposes Haman's plot. Moved by Esther's plea, the king orders Haman's execution. Esther's wise and brave actions lead to the issuing of a new decree that allows the Jews to defend themselves, saving them from annihilation.

UPRIGHT KEYWORDS:	REVERSED KEYWORDS:
Curiosity	Deception
Vigilance	Gossip
Truthfulness	Misunderstanding
Strategic planning	Hastiness
Bravery	Superficiality

CARD MEANING IN UPRIGHT POSITION:

Represents an individual who approaches situations with curiosity and intellect, ready to speak the truth and stand up for what is right. It embodies the use of strategic thinking and bravery to navigate through challenges.

- **Curiosity:** *Seeking knowledge and understanding.*
- **Vigilance:** *Staying alert to potential threats or injustices, ready to act.*
- **Truthfulness:** *Commitment to honesty and using truth to protect and defend.*
- **Strategic Planning:** *Using intellect and foresight to navigate complex situations.*
- **Bravery:** *Showing courage in the face of danger, especially when standing up for others.*

CARD MEANING IN REVERSED POSITION:

Tendency towards haste, superficiality, or using one's intellect in deceitful or harmful ways. It suggests a need for greater understanding and caution to avoid misunderstandings or negative consequences of impulsive actions.

- **Deception:** *Engaging in or falling victim to dishonesty and manipulation.*
- **Gossip:** *Spreading information that can harm others.*
- **Misunderstanding:** *Failing to communicate clearly.*
- **Hastiness:** *Acting without sufficient thought or planning, leading to mistakes.*
- **Superficiality:** *Focusing on the surface without understanding the depth of a situation.*

Esther's story celebrates the impact of strategic thinking, the moral courage to speak truth to power, and the effect of using one's intellect and voice for the greater good, embodying the positive attributes of the "Page of Feathers" while cautioning against the pitfalls of its reversed aspects.

Knight of Feathers

PAUL THE APOSTLE

Saul promptly began to proclaim Jesus in the synagogues, declaring, "He is the Son of God."
Acts 9:20 BSB

Paul, originally named Saul, begins as a persecutor of Christians, zealous in his efforts to uphold Jewish law. On the road to Damascus, intending to arrest more Christians, he is struck by a blinding light and hears the voice of Jesus. This encounter leads to Paul's conversion, after which he becomes one of Christianity's most influential apostles. He undertakes several missionary journeys, faces persecution, and writes many letters that form a significant part of the New Testament, spreading the Christian message with unparalleled zeal and intellectual argumentation.

UPRIGHT KEYWORDS:	REVERSED KEYWORDS:
Zeal	*Fanaticism*
Determination	*Harshness*
Swift action	*Impulsiveness*
Intellectual rigor	*Misdirected energy*
Bold communication	*Confrontation*

CARD MEANING IN UPRIGHT POSITION:

High energy, clarity of purpose, and a drive to pursue goals with determination and intellectual insight. It represents the courage to stand up for one's beliefs and to communicate those beliefs boldly.

- **Zeal:** *Embracing one's mission with passionate intensity.*
- **Determination:** *Facing obstacles with resolve and a clear sense of purpose.*
- **Swift Action:** *Moving quickly to seize opportunities or to advocate for change.*
- **Intellectual Rigor:** *Employing logical and persuasive argumentation to advance one's cause.*
- **Bold Communication:** *Speaking out fearlessly in defense of one's beliefs.*

CARD MEANING IN REVERSED POSITION:

Indicates potential for zeal to turn into fanaticism, where the pursuit of one's ideals may lead to confrontation or the alienation of others. It implies a need to temper passion with consideration for others and to reflect on the direction of one's energy.

- **Fanaticism:** *Allowing zeal to overshadow empathy.*
- **Harshness:** *Communicating in ways that may be perceived as overly aggressive or insensitive.*
- **Impulsiveness:** *Acting without sufficient thought to the consequences.*
- **Misdirected Energy:** *Channeling one's efforts in ways that may not be constructive or beneficial.*
- **Confrontation:** *Engaging in conflicts that stem more from a desire to dominate than to enlighten.*

The "Knight of Feathers" card shows the dual nature of passionate advocacy—its power to inspire and effect change, as well as the importance of mindful action and empathy in the pursuit of one's goals.

Queen of Feathers

ABIGAIL THE PEACEMAKER

Blessed is your discernment, and blessed are you,
because today you kept me from bloodshed
and from avenging myself by my own hand.
1 Samuel 25:33 BSB

Abigail, the wife of Nabal, a wealthy but harsh man, intervenes to prevent bloodshed between her husband and David. After Nabal insultingly refuses to provide food to David and his men, despite their protection of his flock, David vows revenge. Abigail, learning of the impending danger, quickly gathers provisions and sets off to meet David. She offers the supplies and pleads for peace, appealing to David's better nature and his future as king of Israel. Her wisdom and eloquence persuade David to abandon his vengeful plan. Abigail's actions demonstrate remarkable diplomatic acumen and moral integrity.

UPRIGHT KEYWORDS:	REVERSED KEYWORDS:
Clarity	*Manipulation*
Insight	*Harsh criticism*
Diplomacy	*Miscommunication*
Articulate communication	*Coldness*
Integrity	*Bitterness*

CARD MEANING IN UPRIGHT POSITION:

Using of intelligence and clear communication to navigate and resolve conflicts. It represents someone who approaches challenges with insight, empathy, and integrity, wielding truth and understanding as tools for resolution.

- **Clarity:** *Clear understanding of complex situations.*
- **Insight:** *Using deep insight to navigate challenges effectively.*
- **Diplomacy:** *Employing tactful communication to manage and resolve conflicts.*
- **Articulate Communication:** *Speaking truthfully and persuasively to influence outcomes.*
- **Integrity:** *Acting with moral fortitude and honesty.*

CARD MEANING IN REVERSED POSITION:

Misuse of one's intellectual and communicative abilities, such as manipulation or delivering harsh truths without empathy. It suggests a need for warmth and connection to balance one's sharp intellect.

- **Manipulation:** *Using one's intellect and eloquence for selfish or deceitful ends.*
- **Harsh Criticism:** *Delivering truth in a way that is unnecessarily cutting or unkind.*
- **Miscommunication:** *Failing to convey one's message effectively, leading to misunderstandings.*
- **Coldness:** *Detaching emotionally from others.*
- **Bitterness:** *Holding onto grievances, which colors communication negatively.*

Abigail's story underlines the power of articulate and thoughtful communication in resolving conflicts and the importance of acting with integrity and insight. It celebrates the qualities of diplomacy and understanding as pivotal forces for peace, while also acknowledging the challenges inherent in wielding truth and intellect with compassion and grace.

King of Feathers

THE JUDGMENT OF SOLOMON

Then the king gave his ruling:
"Give the living baby to the first woman.
By no means should you kill him; she is his mother."
1 Kings 3:27 BSB

Two women come before King Solomon, each claiming to be the mother of a baby. Solomon suggests cutting the baby in half, each woman to receive half. One woman agrees to the division, but the other, the true mother, pleads for the baby's life, offering to relinquish her claim so that her child may live. Solomon, discerning the true mother's compassion, awards her the baby, demonstrating unparalleled wisdom and understanding of human nature. This story highlights Solomon's ability to govern with insight and justice, earning him a reputation for wisdom.

UPRIGHT KEYWORDS:	REVERSED KEYWORDS:
Wisdom	*Tyranny*
Authority	*Manipulation*
Clarity	*Over-analysis*
Intellectual leadership	*Coldness*
Fair judgment	*Unfairness*

CARD MEANING IN UPRIGHT POSITION:

Represents the embodiment of wisdom, clarity, and the moral high ground in leadership and decision-making. It symbolizes the capacity to use intellect and fairness to navigate complex issues, prioritizing truth and justice.

- **Wisdom:** *Applying deep understanding and insight to make enlightened decisions.*
- **Authority:** *Exercising leadership with integrity.*
- **Clarity:** *Seeing through deception and complexity.*
- **Intellectual Leadership:** *Guiding others through the strength of thought and moral principle.*
- **Fair Judgment:** *Making decisions that are just and considerate of all parties involved.*

CARD MEANING IN REVERSED POSITION:

Misusing intellectual power, leading to decisions that may be overly analytical, lacking in empathy, or unjust. It warns of the dark side of authority when it becomes disconnected from the human element.

- **Tyranny:** *Dominating others through intellectual or authoritative might.*
- **Manipulation:** *Twisting facts or logic to serve one's own ends.*
- **Over-analysis:** *Getting lost in details to the point of missing the larger picture.*
- **Coldness:** *Failing to consider the emotional or human side of decisions.*
- **Unfairness:** *Making biased or unjust decisions.*

Solomon's judgment story illustrates the ideal qualities of the King of Feathers: a leader who wields knowledge and fairness as tools to serve justice, embodying the virtues of discernment and principled decision-making, while also cautioning against the misuse of intellectual authority.

MINOR ARCANA

Grains

Ace of Grains

ENTERING THE PROMISED LAND

I have given you every place where the sole of your foot will tread,
just as I promised to Moses.
Joshua 1:3 BSB

After the death of Moses, Joshua is appointed by God to lead the Israelites into the Promised Land. God commands Joshua to be strong and courageous, promising to be with him as he was with Moses. Joshua is to lead the people across the Jordan River into the land God has promised to their ancestors. This marks a new beginning for the Israelites, a fulfillment of God's promise of a land flowing with milk and honey. It signifies not just a physical relocation but a spiritual inheritance, a foundation upon which the future of the Israelite nation is to be built.

" I will give you every place where you set your foot,
as I promised Moses."
Joshua 1:3 (NIV)

ACE *of* GRAINS
ENTERING THE PROMISED LAND

UPRIGHT KEYWORDS:	REVERSED KEYWORDS:
New opportunities	*Missed opportunities*
Prosperity	*Material loss*
Manifestation	*Lack of planning*
Abundance	*Wastefulness*
Security	*Insecurity*

CARD MEANING IN UPRIGHT POSITION:

Great potential and opportunity for growth and prosperity. It points to the start of a promising venture or the laying down of a solid foundation for future success. The focus is on material gain, security, and the realization of long-term goals.

- **New Opportunities:** *Embarking on a new venture that promises growth and prosperity.*
- **Prosperity:** *The flow of abundance and the realization of material security.*
- **Manifestation:** *Turning dreams and promises into tangible realities.*
- **Abundance:** *Plentiful resources and material wealth.*
- **Security:** *Establishing a stable foundation for future endeavors.*

CARD MEANING IN REVERSED POSITION:

Delays, obstacles, or missteps in achieving material or financial goals. It suggests a need to reevaluate strategies, avoid wastefulness, and guard against missed opportunities or material insecurity.

- **Missed Opportunities:** *Overlooking or failing to seize valuable chances for advancement.*
- **Material Loss:** *Experiencing setbacks or losses that affect financial stability.*
- **Lack of Planning:** *Neglecting necessary preparation, leading to challenges in manifestation.*
- **Wastefulness:** *Mismanaging resources, leading to unnecessary depletion of wealth.*
- **Insecurity:** *Facing uncertainty regarding financial matters or material well-being.*

The "Ace of Grains" highlights the themes of opportunity, security, and the manifestation of blessings, while also acknowledging the challenges and responsibilities that accompany material abundance and the journey towards achieving it.

Two of Grains

LYDIA - FAITHFUL BUSINESSWOMAN

Among those listening was a woman named Lydia, a dealer in purple cloth from the city of Thyatira, who was a worshiper of God. The Lord opened her heart to respond to Paul's message.
Acts 16:14 BSB

"One of those listening was a woman from the city of Thyatira named Lydia, a dealer in purple cloth. She was a worshiper of God."
Acts 16:14 (NIV)

TWO *of* GRAINS
LYDIA - FAITHFUL BUSINESSWOMAN

Lydia, a seller of purple cloth in Philippi, meets Paul and his companions during their missionary travels. She is described as a worshiper of God, and upon hearing Paul's message, she and her household are baptized, embracing Christianity. Demonstrating hospitality and support for Paul's mission, Lydia invites them into her home, providing a base for their work in the city. Her story illustrates the successful integration of professional success and personal faith, showing how her resources and influence support the early Christian community.

UPRIGHT KEYWORDS:	REVERSED KEYWORDS:
Balance	Imbalance
Flexibility	Overwhelm
Adaptability	Financial instability
Resource management	Resistance to change
Integration of dualities	Disconnection

CARD MEANING IN UPRIGHT POSITION:

Successful juggling of responsibilities, opportunities, and resources. It shows the ability to adapt to changes and maintain balance between various aspects of life, including the harmonious integration of material and spiritual pursuits.

- **Balance:** *Successfully managing multiple aspects of life or responsibilities.*
- **Flexibility:** *Adapting to change with ease and resilience.*
- **Adaptability:** *Navigating fluctuations in life or business.*
- **Resource Management:** *Efficiently utilizing available resources for maximum benefit.*
- **Integration of Dualities:** *Harmonizing different areas of life, such as work and faith.*

CARD MEANING IN REVERSED POSITION:

Difficulties in managing multiple responsibilities or the challenges of maintaining balance. Potential situation that can lead to financial stress, resistance to necessary change, or a disconnection between values and actions.

- **Imbalance:** *Struggling to maintain equilibrium between different areas of life.*
- **Overwhelm:** *Feeling burdened by too many obligations.*
- **Financial Instability:** *Experiencing uncertainty or difficulty in financial matters.*
- **Resistance to Change:** *Holding onto the status quo, even when adaptation is needed.*
- **Disconnection:** *Losing sight of one's values or priorities in the face of challenges.*

Lydia's example shows that it's possible to maintain balance and stay true to oneself in all areas of life. She focuses on being adaptable, resourceful, and making sure her actions match her beliefs, even though achieving this balance can be challenging.

Three of Grains

BUILDING SOLOMON'S TEMPLE

"As for this temple you are building, if you walk in My statutes, carry out My ordinances, and keep all My commandments by walking in them, I will fulfill through you the promise I made to your father David.
1 Kings 6:12 BSB

Solomon embarks on the ambitious project of building the temple to house the Ark of the Covenant, fulfilling a divine mandate and his father David's dream. The construction involves skilled artisans, vast resources, and detailed planning, reflecting Solomon's commitment to creating a magnificent space for worship. It symbolizes not only religious devotion but also the power of collective endeavor and expert craftsmanship. The temple's completion after seven years stands as a testament to Solomon's wisdom, the workers' skill, and the nation's collective effort.

UPRIGHT KEYWORDS:	REVERSED KEYWORDS:
Collaboration	*Lack of teamwork*
Craftsmanship	*Poor quality*
Dedication	*Delays*
Achievement	*Miscommunication*
Skillful execution	*Unfulfilled potential*

CARD MEANING IN UPRIGHT POSITION:

Productive collaboration and the pooling of talents to achieve a common goal. It emphasizes the value of hard work, expertise, and dedication to excellence, leading to tangible achievements and the realization of ambitious projects.

- **Collaboration:** *Working harmoniously with others to achieve common goals.*
- **Craftsmanship:** *Applying expert skills and attention to detail in one's work.*
- **Dedication:** *Committing fully to a project or task with the aim of achieving the best outcome.*
- **Achievement:** *Reaching significant milestones through collective effort and expertise.*
- **Skillful Execution:** *Realizing a vision through careful planning and skilled implementation.*

CARD MEANING IN REVERSED POSITION:

Obstacles to successful collaboration, such as miscommunication, lack of coordination, or compromised quality. It warns of the consequences of poor planning or teamwork, potentially leading to incomplete projects or the failure to meet shared objectives.

- **Lack of Teamwork:** *Struggling to unite team members towards a common purpose.*
- **Delays:** *Experiencing setbacks that hinder progress and completion.*
- **Miscommunication:** *Failing to effectively communicate, leading to confusion and errors.*
- **Unfulfilled Potential:** *Missing the opportunity to achieve greatness due to preventable flaws.*

Solomon's temple serves as a symbol of what can be accomplished through unity, dedication, and the pursuit of excellence, while also accentuating the challenges and the value of clear communication and coordination in collaborative endeavors.

Four of Grains

PARABLE OF THE RICH FOOL

And He said to them,
"Watch out! Guard yourselves against every form of greed, for one's
life does not consist in the abundance of his possessions."
Luke 12:15 BSB

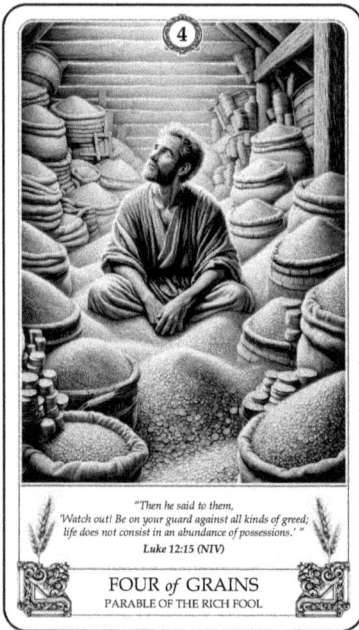

Jesus tells the parable of a rich man who, after a bountiful harvest, decides to tear down his barns to build larger ones to store all his grain and goods. He believes this will secure his future, allowing him to relax, eat, drink, and be merry. However, God calls him a fool because his life is demanded of him that very night, and he cannot take his wealth with him after death. The parable concludes with the lesson that this is how it will be for anyone who stores up treasures for themselves but is not rich toward God.

UPRIGHT KEYWORDS:	REVERSED KEYWORDS:
Security	*Generosity*
Conservatism	*Openness*
Materialism	*Letting go*
Stability	*Financial instability*
Possessiveness	*Reassessment of values*

CARD MEANING IN UPRIGHT POSITION:

Focusing on accumulating and maintaining material wealth and security, potentially to the exclusion of spiritual or emotional growth. It symbolizes the human desire for stability but warns against becoming too attached or conservative in one's financial or material pursuits.

- **Security:** *Seeking financial stability and the assurance that comes with having resources.*
- **Conservatism:** *Adopting a cautious approach to financial matters, possibly avoiding risks.*
- **Materialism:** *Valuing material possessions and wealth above other forms of richness.*
- **Possessiveness:** *Clinging to what one has out of fear of loss or change.*

CARD MEANING IN REVERSED POSITION:

A shift away from strict materialism towards a more generous or open stance. It indicates either a voluntary or enforced reassessment of one's relationship with wealth, highlighting the potential for financial instability or the liberation found in prioritizing non-material values.

- **Generosity:** *Shifting focus towards sharing and giving, finding value in generosity.*
- **Openness:** *Becoming more open to change.*
- **Letting go:** *Releasing the tight grip on possessions and welcoming spiritual abundance.*
- **Financial Instability:** *Facing challenges that test one's material security but open the door to spiritual growth.*
- **Reassessment of Values:** *Evaluating what truly matters beyond the accumulation of wealth.*

The "Four of Grains" invites reflection on the true nature of security and wealth, encouraging a balance between the material and the spiritual, and a recognition of the transient nature of earthly possessions in contrast to the enduring value of generosity, openness, and spiritual growth.

Five of Grains

THE BLEEDING WOMAN

She said to herself,
"If only I touch His cloak, I will be healed."
Matthew 9:21 BSB

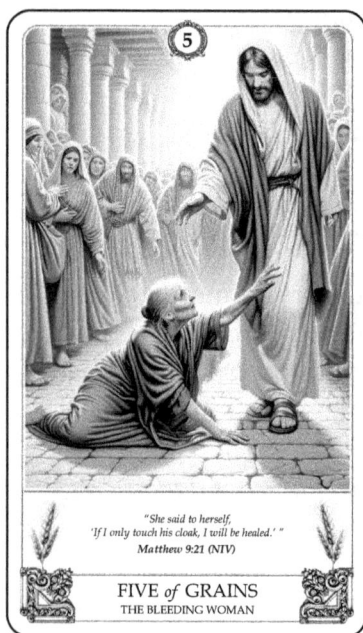

The story tells of a woman who had been bleeding for twelve years, a condition that made her ritually unclean and isolated her from society. Despite spending all she had on treatments without improvement, her situation only worsened. Hearing about Jesus, she approaches Him in a crowd, believing that touching His cloak would heal her. Her faith is rewarded; she touches His garment and is instantly healed. Jesus turns to her and acknowledges her faith, saying, "Daughter, your faith has healed you. Go in peace and be freed from your suffering."

UPRIGHT KEYWORDS:	REVERSED KEYWORDS:
Hardship	*Recovery*
Isolation	*Hope*
Illness	*Reintegration*
Seeking help	*Renewal of faith*
Faith amidst adversity	*Overcoming challenges*

CARD MEANING IN UPRIGHT POSITION:

Period of difficulty, health challenges, or financial hardship, emphasizing feelings of exclusion or desperation. "It shows a need to reach out for help and the importance of faith and perseverance in facing life's adversities."

- **Hardship:** *Enduring difficult circumstances, possibly related to health or financial issues.*
- **Isolation:** *Feeling cut off from others, either socially or emotionally, due to one's struggles.*
- **Illness:** *Dealing with long-term health issues that impact one's quality of life.*
- **Seeking Help:** *The necessity of reaching out for assistance or healing.*
- **Faith amidst Adversity:** *Maintaining hope and belief in the possibility of change despite challenges.*

CARD MEANING IN REVERSED POSITION:

Signals the beginning of recovery from hardship, the rekindling of hope, and the potential for returning to a state of well-being and integration into the community. It indicates a renewal and the positive changes that come with overcoming significant personal trials.

- **Recovery:** *Beginning to heal from illness or emerge from financial difficulty.*
- **Hope:** *Rediscovering optimism and the belief that improvement is possible.*
- **Reintegration:** *Moving towards rejoining community or social circles after a period of isolation.*
- **Overcoming Challenges:** *Finding the strength to surmount obstacles and move forward positively.*

The "Five of Grains" underlines the transformative power of faith, the importance of reaching out for help, and the potential for recovery and reintegration, offering a profound message of hope and resilience in the face of life's hardships.

Six of Grains

WIDOW'S GENEROSITY

Jesus called His disciples to Him and said,
"Truly I tell you, this poor widow has put more than all the others
into the treasury.
Mark 12:43 BSB

"Calling his disciples to him, Jesus said,
'Truly I tell you, this poor widow has put more into
the treasury than all the others.' "
Mark 12:43 (NIV)

SIX *of* GRAINS
WIDOW'S GENEROSITY

Jesus observes people offering money at the temple and notices a poor widow who contributes just a couple small coins, worth very little. He tells His disciples that this widow has given more than all the others making contributions because they gave out of their wealth, but she, out of her poverty, put in everything she had, all she had to live on. This act of selfless giving demonstrates true generosity and sacrifice, contrasting with those who give only from their surplus.

UPRIGHT KEYWORDS:	REVERSED KEYWORDS:
Generosity	*Selfishness*
Charity	*Scarcity mindset*
Kindness	*Hoarding*
Sharing resources	*Inequity*
Equitable distribution	*Exploitation*

CARD MEANING IN UPRIGHT POSITION:

Reflects a spirit of altruism and the importance of giving to those in need, recognizing that true generosity measures not by the amount given but by the spirit and sacrifice behind the gift.

- **Generosity:** *Demonstrating a willingness to give freely.*
- **Charity:** *Engaging in acts of kindness and support for the less fortunate.*
- **Kindness:** *Showing compassion and empathy towards others through actions.*
- **Sharing Resources:** *The equitable distribution of wealth or resources to ensure others' well-being.*
- **Equitable Distribution:** *Ensuring that generosity reaches those who need it most and promoting fairness.*

CARD MEANING IN REVERSED POSITION:

Greed, selfishness, or giving with strings attached. It points to a lack of balance in giving and receiving, where one may either hoard resources out of fear or exploit generosity for personal gain.

- **Selfishness:** *Focusing solely on one's own needs or benefits, at the expense of others.*
- **Scarcity Mindset:** *Operating from a place of fear of lack, leading to hoarding or unwillingness to share.*
- **Hoarding:** *Accumulating resources without thought for the needs of others.*
- **Inequity:** *Contributing to or maintaining unequal distribution of resources.*
- **Exploitation:** *Taking advantage of others' generosity or situations for personal gain.*

This card invites reflection on the nature of our contributions to society and the significance of supporting one another with a genuine heart, illustrating the profound difference made by acts of kindness, regardless of their size, in achieving a more equitable and compassionate world.

Seven of Grains

PARABLE OF THE SOWER

*Others fell on good soil
and yielded fruit: some one hundred times as much,
some sixty, and some thirty.*
Matthew 13:8 WEB

Jesus tells a parable about a sower who scatters seeds. Some seeds fall on the path and are eaten by birds. Some fall on rocky ground and, though they sprout quickly, they wither under the sun's heat because they have no root. Other seeds fall among thorns, which grow up and choke the plants. Finally, some seeds fall on good soil, where they produce a crop multiple times what was sown. Jesus explains that the seeds represent the word of God and the various types of ground symbolize different responses from those who hear the word.

"Still other seed fell on good soil, where it produced a crop – a hundred, sixty or thirty times what was sown."
Matthew 13:8 (NIV)

SEVEN *of* GRAINS
PARABLE OF THE SOWER

UPRIGHT KEYWORDS:	REVERSED KEYWORDS:
Patience	*Frustration*
Investment	*Impatience*
Assessment	*Short-term focus*
Diligence	*Lack of foresight*
Long-term view	*Disappointment*

CARD MEANING IN UPRIGHT POSITION:

Time of hard work and dedication toward a long-term goal, understanding that results take time to manifest. It shows the value of perseverance, planning, and regular assessment of one's progress towards achieving sustainable success.

- **Patience:** *Embracing the waiting period necessary for growth and fruition.*
- **Investment:** *Committing time, energy, and resources to a venture with the expectation of future gain.*
- **Assessment:** *Regularly evaluating the progress and effectiveness of one's efforts.*
- **Diligence:** *Consistently applying oneself to work, with attention to detail and quality.*
- **Long-term View:** *Focusing on sustainable outcomes rather than immediate rewards.*

CARD MEANING IN REVERSED POSITION:

Feelings of frustration or impatience with the pace of progress. It suggests a need to reevaluate one's strategies or expectations, warning against neglecting the quality of preparation and the importance of a steady, focused approach.

- **Frustration:** *Experiencing dissatisfaction with slow progress or outcomes.*
- **Impatience:** *Desiring quick results without sufficient investment or preparation.*
- **Lack of Foresight:** *Failing to plan adequately for future challenges or opportunities.*
- **Disappointment:** *Facing setbacks or failures due to inadequate groundwork or unrealistic expectations.*

The "Seven of Grains" underlines the virtue of patience, and the wisdom of maintaining a long-term perspective in all endeavors, whether they be personal, or professional, while also acknowledging the challenges that can arise when expectations are not met.

Eight of Grains

THE CRAFTSMEN

"So Bezalel, Oholiab, and every skilled person are to carry out everything commanded by the LORD, who has given them skill and ability to know how to perform all the work of constructing the sanctuary."
Exodus 36:1 BSB

God instructs Moses to construct a Tabernacle as a dwelling place for His presence among the Israelites during their journey through the desert. Bezalel of the tribe of Judah and Oholiab of the tribe of Dan are filled with the Spirit of God, granting them wisdom, understanding, and skill in all kinds of crafts. They, along with other skilled artisans, are tasked with building the Tabernacle and its furnishings according to precise specifications given by God. This work not only requires technical skill but also spiritual dedication, as it serves a holy purpose.

UPRIGHT KEYWORDS:	REVERSED KEYWORDS:
Mastery	*Lack of focus*
Dedication	*Mediocrity*
Skill development	*Repetition without progress*
Attention to detail	*Neglecting one's craft*
Pride in one's work	*Dissatisfaction with work*

CARD MEANING IN UPRIGHT POSITION:

Focused skill-building, where hard work and dedication lead to the achievement of high standards. It represents the commitment to one's craft or profession, emphasizing the importance of continuous learning and striving for excellence.

- **Mastery:** *Achieving a high level of skill and expertise in one's field.*
- **Dedication:** *Committing oneself fully to the perfection of one's craft.*
- **Skill Development:** *Actively seeking to learn and improve in all aspects of work.*
- **Attention to Detail:** *Focusing on the minutiae to ensure the highest quality.*
- **Pride in One's Work:** *Taking satisfaction in the fruits of one's labor and effort.*

CARD MEANING IN REVERSED POSITION:

Stagnation or lack of progress.. It warns about a situation where repetition does not lead to improvement, possibly due to a lack of engagement or the neglect of one's skills and potential for growth.

- **Lack of Focus:** *Scattering energy, leading to a failure to advance or refine one's skills.*
- **Mediocrity:** *Settling for average results due to a lack of ambition or effort.*
- **Repetition Without Progress:** *Engaging in work mechanically, without learning or growing.*
- **Dissatisfaction with Work:** *Feeling unfulfilled or disconnected from one's vocational activities.*

The "Eight of Grains" illustrates the rewards of persistence and hard work in achieving excellence, while also cautioning against complacency and the loss of purpose in one's professional and personal endeavors.

Nine of Grains

QUEEN OF SHEBA VISITS SOLOMON

Then she gave the king 120 talents of gold, a great quantity of spices, and precious stones. Never again were spices in such abundance brought in as those the queen of Sheba gave to King Solomon.
1 Kings 10:10 BSB

The Queen of Sheba hears of Solomon's fame and wisdom, which she finds hard to believe, so she decides to visit Jerusalem to test him with hard questions. Solomon answers all her questions, and nothing remains hidden from him. She is overwhelmed by his wisdom, the prosperity of his kingdom, and the happiness of his subjects. Recognizing his wisdom and the blessings of his God, she gifts him gold, spices, and precious stones. Solomon, in turn, grants the queen everything she desires. The visit exemplifies mutual respect and the sharing of wealth and wisdom between two great rulers.

UPRIGHT KEYWORDS:	REVERSED KEYWORDS:
Prosperity	*Materialism*
Wisdom	*Overindulgence*
Self-sufficiency	*Self-satisfaction*
Achievement	*Isolation*
Luxury	*Missed spiritual wealth*

CARD MEANING IN UPRIGHT POSITION:

Self-achieved prosperity and contentment, where one's hard work, wisdom, and diligence have led to a comfortable and luxurious life. It symbolizes not only financial wealth but also intellectual and emotional satisfaction.

- **Prosperity:** *Enjoying the fruits of one's labor and the accumulation of wealth.*
- **Wisdom:** *Valuing and utilizing knowledge and understanding in all aspects of life.*
- **Self-sufficiency:** *Achieving a level of independence and security through one's own efforts.*
- **Achievement:** *Recognizing and celebrating one's successes and accomplishments.*
- **Luxury:** *Experiencing the comfort and pleasures that wealth can provide.*

CARD MEANING IN REVERSED POSITION:

Pitfalls of wealth, such as becoming overly focused on material gain at the expense of spiritual or personal growth. It may also indicate feelings of isolation due to one's wealth or achievements, or the negative aspects of indulgence and complacency.

- **Materialism:** *Placing too high a value on material wealth at the expense of deeper values.*
- **Overindulgence:** *Losing oneself in the pleasures of wealth to the detriment of health or moral standing.*
- **Isolation:** *Experiencing loneliness or detachment due to one's wealth or status.*
- **Missed spiritual wealth:** *Overlooking the importance of spiritual or emotional fulfillment in the pursuit of material success.*

The "Nine of Grains" encourages a balanced view of success, acknowledging the virtue of intellectual, emotional, and spiritual wealth alongside material abundance.

Ten of Grains

GOD'S PROMISE TO ABRAHAM

...for all the land that you see,
I will give to you and your offspring forever.
Genesis 13:15 BSB

Abram (later known as Abraham) and Lot, journeying together, find that the land cannot support both their flocks and herdsmen, leading to strife. Abram proposes that they separate to avoid conflict, offering Lot the first choice of the land. Lot chooses the fertile plains of Jordan, while Abram dwells in the land of Canaan. God then promises Abram that his descendants will be as numerous as the stars in the sky and that all the land he sees will be given to him and his offspring forever, establishing the foundation for a lasting legacy.

UPRIGHT KEYWORDS:	REVERSED KEYWORDS:
Wealth	*Disruption*
Legacy	*Conflict over Wealth*
Prosperity	*Broken promises*
Family harmony	*Instability*
Long-term success	*Short-term gain*

CARD MEANING IN UPRIGHT POSITION:

Wise decisions leading to sustained prosperity and security. It emphasizes the importance of harmony within the family or community and the blessings of a legacy that benefits future generations.

- **Wealth:** *Enjoying the fruits of one's labor, resulting in material abundance.*
- **Legacy:** *Building something of lasting value to be passed down through generations.*
- **Prosperity:** *Achieving a state of financial security and abundant resources.*
- **Family Harmony:** *Maintaining peaceful and supportive relationships within the family or community.*
- **Long-term Success:** *Making decisions with a view toward enduring stability and prosperity.*

CARD MEANING IN REVERSED POSITION:

Challenges to financial stability or family unity, possibly due to greed, poor planning, or conflicts. It warns against actions that may compromise long-term security in favor of immediate gratification.

- **Disruption:** *Experiencing challenges that threaten the continuity of one's legacy.*
- **Conflict over Wealth:** *Experiencing strife within the family or community over resources or inheritance.*
- **Broken Promises:** *Dealing with the fallout from unfulfilled commitments or expectations.*
- **Instability:** *Lacking a secure foundation, leading to uncertainty for oneself and one's family.*
- **Short-term Gain:** *Prioritizing immediate benefits at the expense of long-term prosperity and legacy.*

The story of Abram and Lot highlights the balance between immediate needs and long-term goals, underscoring the value of harmony and thoughtful stewardship in building a lasting foundation of wealth and success.

Page of Grains

PRISCILLA - TEACHING THE TEACHERS

And he began to speak boldly in the synagogue. When Priscilla and Aquila heard him, they took him aside and explained to him the way of God more accurately.
Acts 18:26 BSB

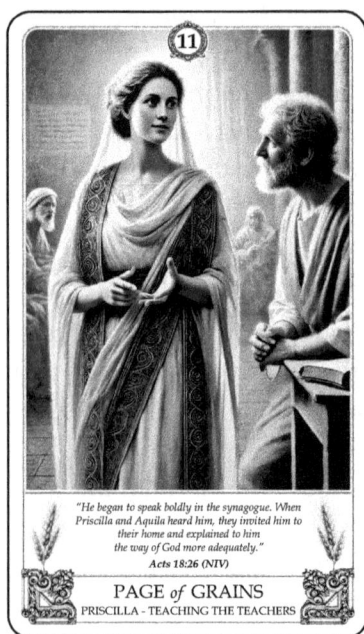

Priscilla and her husband Aquila, tentmakers by trade, meet Paul in Corinth. They work and minister alongside Paul, becoming his close friends and fellow tentmakers. When Paul leaves Corinth, Priscilla and Aquila accompany him to Ephesus. There, they encounter Apollos, who was a persuasive speaker and well-versed in the Scriptures, yet he did not have full understanding of certain matters. Priscilla and Aquila privately guided Apollos, providing him with a more precise understanding of God's teachings. Through their mentorship, Apollos becomes a powerful advocate for Christianity.

UPRIGHT KEYWORDS:	REVERSED KEYWORDS:
Learning	*Procrastination*
Opportunity	*Lack of direction*
Diligence	*Missed opportunities*
Practical application	*Underestimation of abilities*
Mentorship	*Neglect of development*

CARD MEANING IN UPRIGHT POSITION:

Reflects a time of learning and growth, where opportunities for development are embraced with diligence and a practical mindset. It portrays a journey toward mastery or the application of skills in meaningful ways.

- **Learning:** *Embracing new knowledge and skills with enthusiasm and an open mind.*
- **Opportunity:** *Recognizing and seizing chances for growth and improvement.*
- **Diligence:** *Consistently making an effort to learn and improve oneself.*
- **Practical Application:** *Using newly acquired skills in practical, useful ways.*
- **Growth:** *Evolving in one's abilities and understanding through steady effort.*

CARD MEANING IN REVERSED POSITION:

Procrastination, lack of clear direction, or failure to seize opportunities. It implies a need to reevaluate one's approach to personal development or education.

- **Procrastination:** *Delaying or avoiding work or study.*
- **Lack of Direction:** *Uncertainty about which path to take for personal or professional development.*
- **Missed Opportunities:** *Overlooking or failing to take advantage of chances to learn or advance.*
- **Underestimation of Abilities:** *Doubting one's potential to learn new skills or improve.*
- **Neglect of Development:** *Ignoring the need for ongoing education and skill enhancement.*

Priscilla's example illustrates the importance of lifelong learning, teaching, and the positive impact these endeavors have on individual growth and community support, while also cautioning against the pitfalls that can prevent personal and communal advancement.

Knight of Grains

JACOB WORKS FOR LABAN

So Jacob served seven years for Rachel,
yet it seemed but a few days because of his love for her.
Genesis 29:20 BSB

> *"So Jacob served seven years to get Rachel, but they seemed like only a few days to him because of his love for her."*
> *Genesis 29:20 (NIV)*

KNIGHT *of* GRAINS
JACOB WORKS FOR LABAN

Jacob flees to his uncle Laban's house after deceiving his brother Esau. Upon arriving, Jacob falls in love with Laban's younger daughter, Rachel, and agrees to work for Laban for seven years to marry her. However, Laban deceives Jacob by giving him his older daughter Leah instead, requiring Jacob to serve another seven years for Rachel. Jacob's commitment and hard work over these years, and even beyond, for the wealth he eventually acquires, reflect his determination and resilience.

UPRIGHT KEYWORDS:	REVERSED KEYWORDS:
Persistence	*Stagnation*
Reliability	*Lack of progress*
Hard work	*Inflexibility*
Patience	*Missed opportunities*
Goal-oriented	*Overcautiousness*

CARD MEANING IN UPRIGHT POSITION:

Commitment to a task or goal, emphasizing the virtues of patience, reliability, and the gradual achievement of objectives through consistent effort.

- **Persistence:** *Demonstrating unwavering dedication to achieving a specific aim.*
- **Reliability:** *Being dependable and steady in one's efforts and commitments.*
- **Hard Work:** *Committing to one's duties and responsibilities with diligence and effort.*
- **Patience:** *Exhibiting patience over long periods to realize one's goals.*
- **Goal-oriented:** *Focusing on and working steadily towards long-term objectives.*

CARD MEANING IN REVERSED POSITION:

Challenges related to becoming too fixed in one's methods or too cautious in pursuit of goals, leading to stagnation or the failure to seize opportunities for growth.

- **Stagnation:** *Experiencing a lack of growth or advancement due to overly cautious approach.*
- **Lack of Progress:** *Failing to move forward or improve despite efforts.*
- **Inflexibility:** *Being unwilling or unable to adapt to new circumstances or opportunities.*
- **Missed Opportunities:** *Overlooking chances for advancement or change due to fear or complacency.*
- **Overcautiousness:** *Hesitating to take risks that could lead to growth or success.*

Jacob's story demonstrates the value of perseverance and reliability in reaching one's goals, while also serving as a cautionary tale about the risks of rigidity and the potential costs of undervalued work and personal sacrifice.

Queen of Grains

PROVERBS 31 WOMAN

She perceives that her merchandise is profitable.
Her lamp doesn't go out by night.
Proverbs 31:18 WEB

"She sees that her trading is profitable,
and her lamp does not go out at night."
Proverbs 31:18 (NIV)

QUEEN *of* GRAINS
PROVERBS 31 WOMAN

Proverbs 31 describes an ideal woman who is virtuous and capable, known for her strong character, wisdom, and industrious nature. She is a diligent homemaker, a savvy businesswoman, and a provider for her family, making her a pillar of strength and stability. Her actions are driven by love and care, and she is respected by her family and community. This passage highlights the value of a woman who fears the Lord and showcases her roles in both the domestic and economic spheres with excellence.

UPRIGHT KEYWORDS:	REVERSED KEYWORDS:
Resourcefulness	*Neglect*
Nurturing	*Materialism*
Stability	*Overburdened*
Prosperity	*Lack of care*
Practical wisdom	*Mismanagement*

CARD MEANING IN UPRIGHT POSITION:

Nurturing abundance, where practicality and care converge to create a stable and prosperous environment. It depicts someone who utilizes their resources wisely, offering support and security to those around them.

- **Resourcefulness:** *Excelling in making the most out of available resources.*
- **Nurturing:** *Providing care and support, ensuring the well-being of others.*
- **Stability:** *Creating a secure and dependable environment.*
- **Prosperity:** *Achieving success through hard work and practical skills.*
- **Practical Wisdom:** *Using knowledge and understanding daily to benefit oneself and others..*

CARD MEANING IN REVERSED POSITION:

Difficulties in managing one's resources or priorities, leading to feelings of being overburdened or to the neglect of essential duties. It warns against the pitfalls of materialism or the misallocation of one's energies.

- **Neglect:** *Failing to attend to the needs of oneself or others.*
- **Materialism:** *Focusing too much on material wealth to the detriment of spiritual or emotional well-being.*
- **Overburdened:** *Taking on too much, leading to stress or a decrease in effectiveness.*
- **Mismanagement:** *Poor handling of resources, leading to instability or loss.*

The "Queen of Grains" invites reflection on the idea of balancing material success with the nurturing of family and community, emphasizing the value of wisdom and practical skills in achieving a fulfilling and harmonious life.

King of Grains

JOSEPH IN CHARGE OF EGYPT

Pharaoh also told Joseph,
"I hereby place you over all the land of Egypt."
Genesis 41:41 BSB

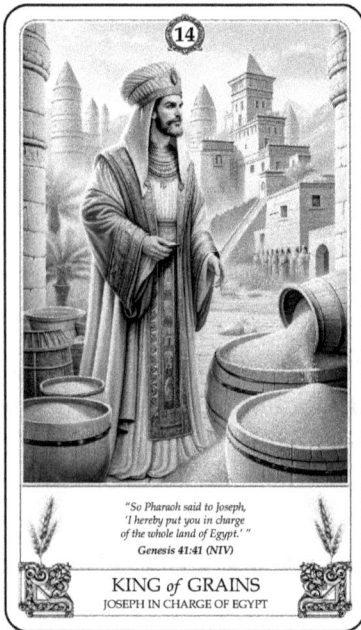

Joseph, sold into slavery by his brothers, rises to prominence in Egypt through his ability to interpret Pharaoh's dreams, which foretell seven years of abundance followed by seven years of famine. Recognizing Joseph's wisdom, Pharaoh puts him in charge of Egypt's land, tasking him with storing grain during the abundant years to prepare for the famine. Joseph's strategic planning and management save not only Egypt but also the surrounding nations from starvation, ultimately leading to a reunion and reconciliation with his family.

UPRIGHT KEYWORDS:	REVERSED KEYWORDS:
Leadership	Mismanagement
Prosperity	Greed
Responsibility	Short-sightedness
Strategic planning	Stubbornness
Resourcefulness	Waste

CARD MEANING IN UPRIGHT POSITION:

Material success and stability through wise leadership, strategic foresight, and responsible management. It describes someone who uses their skills and resources to build prosperity not only for themselves but for the community.

- **Leadership:** *Exemplifying strong leadership qualities and guiding others toward success.*
- **Prosperity:** *Achieving a high level of material and financial success.*
- **Responsibility:** *Taking on the duty to manage resources wisely for the greater good.*
- **Strategic Planning:** *Using foresight and planning to navigate through challenges.*
- **Resourcefulness:** *Finding innovative solutions to problems, ensuring abundance and security.*

CARD MEANING IN REVERSED POSITION:

Mismanagement of resources, greed, or a failure to plan for the future. It warns against the misuse of power or wealth at the expense of others' well-being.

- **Mismanagement:** *Poor handling of resources, leading to loss and instability.*
- **Greed:** *Allowing the desire for wealth to override ethical considerations and the welfare of others.*
- **Short-sightedness:** *Failing to plan for the long term, risking future prosperity for immediate gain.*
- **Stubbornness:** *Refusing to adapt strategies or listen to advice, potentially leading to downfall.*

The "King of Grains" portrays the virtues of leadership, the wisdom of planing, and the importance of using one's position and resources to ensure the well-being of many. It underscores the potential of sound resource management to avert crisis and foster prosperity, while also cautioning against the dangers of mismanagement and greed.

CHAPTER 6

Epilogue

As we turn the final pages of our exploration, we find ourselves standing at the threshold of a new understanding, where ancient wisdom meets personal insight in a dance of spiritual enlightenment. This journey through the symbolic and narrative landscapes of the Biblical Tarot has not merely been an academic exercise but a pilgrimage of the soul, seeking to connect deeper truths with the lived experiences of every seeker who dares to embark on this path.

The Biblical Tarot, in its essence, serves as a bridge between two worlds often seen as disparate: the divine inspiration of the scriptures and the introspective guidance of the tarot. Through this harmonious blend, we've discovered a rich tapestry of spiritual insight, where the archetypal journeys of biblical characters mirror our own quests for understanding, growth, and connection with the divine.

In weaving together the stories of the Bible with the symbolism of the Tarot, we've been invited to see beyond the surface, to the underlying currents of human experience that unite us all. Each card, each story, has offered a lens through which to view the complexities of our lives, encouraging us to reflect, to question, and to grow.

But this is not an ending; it is an invitation. An invitation to continue your exploration, to integrate these insights into your daily practice, and to allow the wisdom of the Biblical Tarot to illuminate your path. The journey of spiritual exploration is ongoing, a perpetual unfolding of understanding and discovery that does not conclude with the last word written here.

As you move forward, armed with the knowledge and inspiration gleaned from these pages, remember that the true power of the Biblical Tarot lies not in the cards themselves but in the connection they foster between you and the divine, between your earthly journey and the spiritual lessons that guide it. Let the stories of the past enrich your present, and may your path be illuminated by the light of wisdom that shines from the fusion of these timeless spiritual tools.

Biblical Tarot opens a doorway to a deeper dialogue with the divine, a conversation that continues with each card drawn and every scripture pondered. May your journey through this sacred synthesis be a source of guidance, comfort, and inspiration as you navigate the unfolding path of your life.

And so, with hearts open and spirits attuned, we step into the future, guided by the light of ancient wisdom, walking a path paved with the insights of the Biblical Tarot. The journey continues, and the story unfolds, ever inviting us to deeper understanding and closer communion with the divine mystery at the heart of all things.

Thank you!